ROSE
BASICS

ROSE

Publishing Director: Laura Bamford
Creative Director: Keith Martin
Executive Editor: Julian Brown
Editor: Karen O'Grady
Executive Art Editor: Mark Winwood
Design: Rozelle Bentheim
Picture Research: Sally Claxton
Production Controller: Clare Smedley
Special Photography: Sean Myers
Illustrator: Vana Haggerty

First published in Great Britain in 1999
by Hamlyn, an imprint of
Octopus Publishing Group Limited
2-4 Heron Quays, London, E14 4JP

A catalogue record for this book is available from the British Library

Produced by Toppan Printing Co., (H.K) Ltd
Printed in Hong Kong

BASICS

Amanda Beales

Hamlyn

Contents

Introduction

Roses are available in an abundance of colours, styles, shapes and sizes; many are scented; some are prickly; and some are thornless. There are roses that should be grown just for the ornamental value of their hips and for their autumn foliage. There are those that benefit the garden by sprawling close to the ground, others that will reach the highest branches of the tallest trees. Some roses date from thousands of years ago, in fact a few have real historical significance, and there are those that have only recently been introduced. Miniature roses, bush roses, climbers, ramblers, scramblers, different types of standard roses, Species roses – the list goes on. Some are pruned after flowering, some in the winter, and a few are best not pruned at all. They can be grown from cuttings, from seed, by being budded or grafted. Some are more prone to disease than others, and there are many different ways of coping with pests and diseases. No wonder gardeners think that roses are confusing!

This book aims to redress this myth and to demonstrate, in simple terms, that roses can actually be quite easy to grow. Indeed, I hope that after reading the pages that follow you will feel confident, not daunted, about growing them. Roses are tremendously rewarding plants, and understanding them makes them even more so. It is my wish that you and the other readers of this book will take one step at a time, instead of rushing out, buying a rose and expecting it to fulfil your every desire. As for the roses you already possess, read, digest the information, then look at them from a new perspective. Either overcome any problems you have with them, or learn to enjoy them even with their problems.

Previously unnoticed foibles may become apparent. If this is the case, do not be alarmed; if your roses have coped so far, they are likely to continue to do so.

For my entire life roses have been like the wallpaper, a most beautiful living wallpaper, always around me, for my father is one of the world's most respected authorities on roses today. The business he heads, and that my brother and I are part of, comprises an important percentage of my life's very existence. The business is very successful, but this was not always the case, for, as they say, from little acorns big oaks grow. As a child, I have happy memories of helping my mother with the watering, and of chatting with the old gentleman who did the budding in the field at the top of our small nursery, 'Uncle Eddie', with his flat cap and his Norfolk drawl. As well as absorbing my parents' ideas and aspirations, it was listening to him and his fellow colleagues, happy in their work, and meeting others 'hooked' on roses that inspired me at an early age. Over the years I have continued to find roses uplifting. Not only do I enjoy their beauty and being near them, I love to indulge in their individual characteristics. I enjoy learning what one variety may do against another, at a particular time. With roses no one can ever know it all.

To me, roses make a garden complete. I hope that, after reading this book, you too will feel the confidence and inspiration to experiment with them in your garden.

Amanda Beale

the anatomy of a bare root rose

NODE
The place at which
leaves and new
shoots form.

PRIMARY STEM
These make up the original
skeleton shape of a plant and
will produce lateral branches.

UNION
The place where the branches and roots
meet. This is the spot where the bud was
originally placed and is therefore often
gnarled in appearance.

FIBROUS ROOT
Hairy roots take in the moisture
and nourishment from the soil.

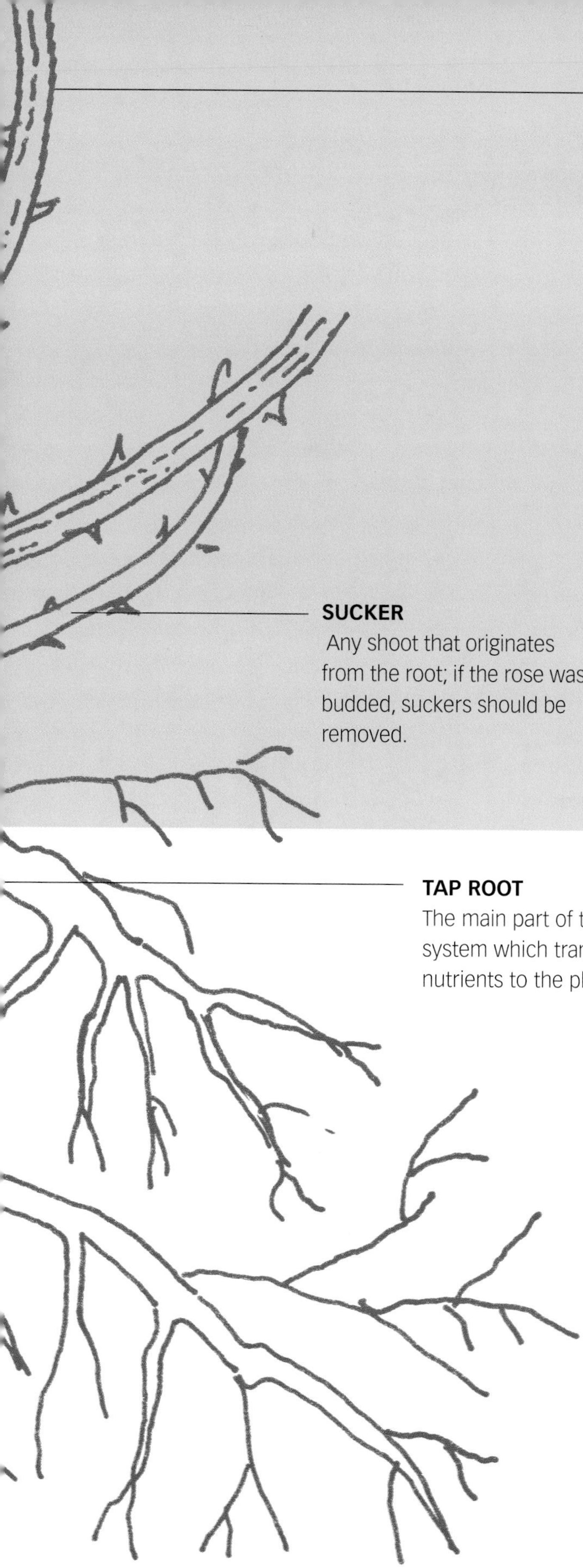

SUCKER
Any shoot that originates
from the root; if the rose was
budded, suckers should be
removed.

TAP ROOT
The main part of the root
system which transport
nutrients to the plant.

All roses fall into the same genus, but can be divided into smaller groups. The 'family' group membership may be far ranging, from bush to climber, from white flower to red, but each rose will portray some similar features, whether cosmetic or physical.

Knowing a little about the history and tendencies of each group helps narrow down the options when choosing new roses for the garden. Also, the final chapter in the book, entitled *Roses for Particular Situations*, gives some ideas of varieties for a range of different situations in the garden (*see* p. 106).

Family Groups

1

Shrub Roses

Albas

The Albas are one of the oldest races of the rose, dating as far back as the 15th century. They are also exquisitely beautiful with grey-green leaves and pastel-shaded flowers. Highly perfumed, they bloom *en masse* in mid-summer. They are extremely healthy, growing to an average 5ft (1.5m) high with quite dense growth. The variety 'Alba Maxima' with fully double flowers is believed to be the 'White Rose of York' adopted by Edward Duke of York, later Edward IV, as the symbol of his House after he had defeated the Lancastrians at Mortimer's Cross in 1461.

Albas: 'Celestial'

Bourbons

The Bourbons are named after their place of origin, the Ile de Bourbon, an island in the southern Indian Ocean. This diverse family ranges from shrubs of around 3ft (1m) to vigorous climbers of 12ft (4m). Flowers from a varied palette are usually scented, some heavily, and are generally double in formation. Most repeat or continue to flower throughout the summer months and often into autumn. This is a reliable family with some very famous varieties among its members.

Centifolias: 'Fantin Latour'

Centifolias

The 'Roses of a hundred petals', also known as the Provence Roses, date from the 15th and 16th centuries. They are the full-faced, blowsy roses so often found in the works of the Old Masters, where they appear absolutely gorgeous, but these portrayals are aesthetic, and lead us to forget that some Centifolias can be cumbersome in growth and difficult to situate in the garden. If long, thorny and arching branches can be coped with, the larger varieties often do bear beautiful shaggy, highly perfumed blooms, although they will require some support. The smaller Centifolias, are often quite neat, with flowers more in proportion to their size.

Chinas

As one might guess, these roses originated in China, where it is thought they existed as early as the 10th century, possibly before. They were later used extensively in hybridisation programmes, at which point they became largely responsible for the long flowering period of most of today's modern roses. Very free flowering, Chinas come in a wide range of colours, and many are highly perfumed. They can be used as bedding in mixed or even specimen planting, but do remember that they are not the hardiest of roses, and will need some form of protection in colder areas. In places where it is just too cold for them to grow them outdoors, they make rewarding greenhouse or conservatory plants.

Chinas: 'Old Blush'

Damasks: 'Ispahan'

Damasks

The Damasks are a very old family of roses, a family prized for its scent in the Middle East where they were used for the extraction of attar to produce perfume. It is not known when Damasks first came to Europe, but they were around in Roman times. This is not the largest family of roses, although there are some beautiful members of it, ranging in colour from mid-pink to white. Most flower just once with one or two exceptions, in particular 'Quatre Saisons' which has a good second flush of flowers. They are a generally healthy and robust group of roses which are probably best placed in the rose or mixed shrubbery.

The English Roses

A race of mixed progeny, the phrase 'New English Roses' was first adopted to market roses which are a mixture of old and new; the word 'New' is now not generally used. They combine the old-fashioned look of roses such as the Gallicas and Bourbons, with modern growth habits and freedom of flower, and are usually perfumed. Most are strong growing with the occasional tendency to be a little lax and willowy. Largely healthy, there are one or two with an annoying proneness to disease, as is the case with most roses. With careful selection an English Rose makes an attractive specimen plant, as well as being equally happy used in bedding or the in shrubbery. Although there are tall English Roses the majority reach a height of 3-4ft (1-1.2m). In my opinion, they benefit from hard pruning to stop them becoming top heavy and, as with all continuous-flowering cultivars, need regular dead-heading to perpetuate blooming.

Gallicas

It is largely believed that the crusaders from the 12th and 13th centuries carried roses from the East to Europe, many of them probably being Gallicas. It is known that the Persians had a Gallica as a religious emblem at least 1,200 years before Christ. Rosa gallica officinallis was one of the roses used by apothecaries in the Middle Ages, in fact is often listed even now as 'The Apothecary's Rose'. It is also the Red Rose of Lancaster adopted by Henry IV as the symbol of his House. These roses were later to become the passion of the Empress Josephine who was said to have collected over 150

varieties. Such is the greatness of these beautiful roses that every garden should have one. Gallicas encompass shades of blush pink through to the deepest maroons and purples and most have outstanding perfumes. On the whole they are generally tidy plants, carrying only a few thorns. The flowers are anything from single to large and fully double. They flower in great abundance in mid-summer and, because most are tolerant of poor soil, they are at home almost anywhere.

The English Roses: 'Graham Thomas'

Gallicas: 'Rosa Mundi'

Hybrid Musks: 'Buff Beauty'

Hybrid Musks

Originally called Pemberton Roses after the Reverend Joseph Pemberton who bred them between 1913 and 1926, Hybrid Musks were the first really neatly proportioned, continuous-flowering cluster roses. Pemberton's varieties remain popular even today, and are indeed excellent roses. The majority of Hybrid Musks available are those created by Pemberton, but there are a few others, introduced after his death, which have also stood the test of time. In colour and form of flower they are quite varied from creamy-white single blooms to flamboyant red and fully double. Most are scented. Hybrid Musks are extremely accommodating; the smaller varieties adapt well to growing in tubs, while some of the larger members of this group can be encouraged to act as small climbers when grown against a wall. The majority even suffer shade and poor soil. At their best, they are an excellent all-encompassing family.

Hybrid Perpetuals

Whilst not totally perpetual, this group of roses will usually supply at least one second flush of flower each year. Most date from the early 1800's, the ancestors of modern-day Hybrid Teas; this influence is clearly displayed in size and shape of flower. The Hybrid Perpetuals reached the height of their popularity in the Victorian era, when big was most definitely beautiful. I value that enthusiasm for these roses; they are big in bloom, sumptuous in fact, and very beautiful. In size, they vary considerably from tidy compact plants to those with more vigorous growth, but in nearly every example well-endowed flowers give away equally well-endowed perfumes. Health varies from plant to plant, but they are not weak. Hybrid Perpetuals are best as companions to other roses or shrubs, but, even if you only have a balcony, there are one or two that lend themselves to being grown in a pot.

Hybrid Teas (The Older Varieties)

A huge family, the Hybrid Teas have been around for many, many years, the first 'La France' having been introduced in 1865. Today, we refer to roses as being either 'old fashioned' or 'modern': Gallicas are old fashioned, miniatures are modern. So where do the Hybrid Teas belong, a group spanning more than a century? Experts give different answers to this question, and I will not bore by repeating them all. Suffice it to say that the Second World War saw a large drop in the numbers introduced; with the advantage of hindsight, the early 1940's appear the ideal chronological cut-off date between 'old-fashioned' and 'modern' Hybrid Teas. The older varieties share very similar characteristics in the form of large, pointed, solitary blooms, borne at the end of a long stem. However, the Victorian craving for 'big and beautiful' did not suit the Hybrid Teas as well as it did the Hybrid Perpetuals. In order to create bigger flowers, they overlooked the health, vigour and perfume of their early introductions, leaving,their inheritors with inferior plants. This is not true of all the older Hybrid Teas, but it takes a real devotee to add some of them to the rose garden. Amongst their ranks, are some wonderful roses: good growers with big perfumes and big flowers. Check the catalogues and the rose dictionaries before deciding which is best for you.

What can be agreed is that Hybrid Teas will not outgrow their welcome, seldom getting above 4ft (1.2m); they will flower continuously (requiring a heavy annual prune); and they are ideal cut flowers.

Modern Shrub Roses

They are called 'Modern Shrub Roses' because they are of such mixed parentage that there is no one particular group with which they have strong affinity. They are indeed a mixed bunch with few similarities except that they largely possess the qualities strived for by modern hybridists: health and freedom of flower. Colours, styles, size and type of flower are across the board. Some are scented, some not very much. Most grow to above 3ft (1m) and some can be adapted to climb in the right situation. In short. by scouring the ranks of the Modern Shrub Roses, there is a variety for every situation and taste.

Modern Shrub Roses: 'Macmillan Nurse'

Moss Roses: 'William Lobb'

Moss Roses

This is a beautiful group of roses. Not only are the flowers an attraction, the stems and unopened buds are as well. These roses are endowed with moss-like glands, which, when touched, have a wonderful herb-like fragrance. In some cases the moss is so prominent that it will catch the eye of any passer-by; such is the case with 'Chapeau de Napoléon',

Pimpinellifolias: 'Altaica'

also called 'Crested Moss', which has buds so heavily covered they resemble Napoleon's hat. Once open, the flowers too are most attractive, as well as being scented. Although separately classified as Moss Roses, this group really belongs to the Centifolias. They are the result of a mutation that occurred early in the 19th-century. Rosa Centifolia Muscosa, a sport of Rosa Centifolia; led to the foundations and breeding programmes which followed; further research added numerous others. There are several with abundant, soft moss rather like 'Chapeau de Napoléon', but also some with no more than high-density thorns. If it were not for the novelty appeal of the moss, there are varieties which would long since have been discarded, but every rose has its place. One of the most garden-worthy Moss Roses is 'Alfred de Dalmas', a rose with many virtues: scent, strong growth, continuous flowering and above all a beautiful blush-pink flower. It is probably more strongly related to the Damasks, as are a few other Mosses, and is one of the few happy to live in a pot. Most others will be more at home in the shrub-rose border or in a wilder, natural planting.

Pimpinellifolias

Native to Europe, this is a tough little bunch of roses. They are prickly, dense and compact with many tiny serrated leaflets. The flowers are small, except in the case of one or two hybrids, appearing in abundance in early summer. The display is not long lived, usually only for about three weeks, but most produce wonderful rotund mahogany-coloured hips in the autumn. They will grow almost anywhere, even in poor soil

Polyanthas: 'Margo Koster'

and in shade, and will cope with most winters. Their tidy growth and density makes Pimpinellifolias ideal candidates for the shorter boundary hedge where sharp thorns will provide a good deterrent to intruders.

Polyanthas

Very popular in the early 1900's these small-flowered, low-growing roses have many uses. They are accommodating enough to grow in pots on the patio or balcony, make good edging to the rose border, as well as being useful bedding. Blooms are borne in clusters and appear freely over a long period. Sometimes listed alongside Floribundas, the Polyanthas tend to be shorter with larger trusses of smaller flowers. They are probably not the best choice for poor soil, but some varieties will tolerate shade.

Portlands

This small family consists of some of the most beautiful old roses. Repeat flowering and usually well scented, with a neat, stocky growth habit, the Portlands are good choices for even the smallest garden. The neat proportions of even the larger ones allow them to grow well in pots where space is limited or they can be employed in hedging or group planting. Whilst a shady situation is not a good idea, most will tolerate all but the very worst soil. The flowers in shades of white through to magenta, often bear many petals and expensive fragrances.

Portlands: 'Rose de Rescht'

Procumbents
(Ground-cover roses)

The term 'ground-cover' is used commonly for different garden plants, but there are not many roses that truly cover the ground in the way this title implies. Instead, I prefer the title, adopted by my father, of Procumbent roses, describing their arching, wide-growing habit much better. Their uses are manifold, from spilling down banks and hiding unsightly manhole covers to tumbling over walls; some are even happy in hanging baskets. In the right position, they can be encouraged to climb, while the larger varieties easily grow into established hedges providing colour and density in growth. Most Procumbents have small flowers in all sorts of colours, and some are scented.

Rugosas

These are some of the toughest roses. Rugosas are thorny and dense with disease-resistant leathery foliage. Flowers, which appear repeatedly throughout the summer, are, in many varieties, followed by splendid hips, often of giant proportion. Accompanying the hips, the leaves adopt various attractive hues in the autumn – a stunningly beautiful combination. Rugosa cultivars are rewarding even in difficult conditions; they make excellent sturdy hedges; and they are extremely good candidates for the mixed shrubbery.

Procumbents: 'Bonica'

Species

These are the wild or true roses of nature, and as such the forerunners to all modern-day hybrids. Nearly all have single flowers and hips of different shapes and sizes. They are healthy roses and are, in the main, hardy. The Species is a diverse group because they are largely unrelated; therefore each has its own fairly distinct characteristics. Some flower early, others later but very few have more than one flush; there are tall and short specimens with different hues and shapes of leaves. Species are at home in the wild garden or natural settings of park and woodland; they also make good hedging; and are worth growing for the ornamental value of their hips (which look great when cut and arranged with other berries and grasses).

Sweet Briars

Derived from Rosa eglanteria, these roses, have wonderful apple-scented foliage which is strongest from young tender shoots. This scent is not always noticeable without touching the leaves but it pervades the air after rain or on dewy mornings. One of the best known is 'Lady Penzance', named for the wife of Lord Penzance, who in the late 1800's bred many of the varieties available in catalogues today. There are one or two repeat-flowering Sweet Briars, but they are hybrids and tend not to have the perfumed leaves; the others bear just one flush of flowers followed by hips in the autumn. The Sweet Briars are perfect in natural settings or in conservation areas, but are also adaptable enough to use in most gardens, where they are best in a setting of other shrubs and roses.

Teas

Not the hardiest of roses, Teas are well worth growing because there are some very beautiful, heavily scented cultivars. In a cold area, it is wise to give these roses some protection in winter, or to grow them in pots so that they can be over-wintered in a cool greenhouse or conservatory. If they have a fault, it is a sparseness of foliage and somewhat lax growth, but I for one can overlook that. They originated in the East where Sir Abraham Hume discovered Rosa indica odorata, now more frequently known as 'Hume's Blush', in 1810. More followed quickly and were thought to have been transported to Europe aboard ships belonging to the East India Tea Company, hence their name.

Sweet Briars: 'Amy Robsart'

Modern Bedding Roses

Hybrid Teas or Large-Flowered Roses

The correct title for this group of roses is a contentious subject. Early Hybrid Teas were exactly that – hybrids of the Tea roses, but over the years the genealogy became complicated. They were recently reclassified as Large-Flowered Roses, but this is often ignored. Having grown up with Hybrid Teas I find it difficult to think of them as anything else. Whatever title you choose, this is a huge family. They usually bear solitary blooms, ideal for the flower arranger, although a few produce small clusters. Within their ranks are colours for every taste, many boasting a perfume. Generally they are quite short, bushy and free flowering over a long period. Their use in the garden is manifold. They are ideal in pots for balconies and patios, especially when under-planted with trailing annuals. *En masse* Hybrid Teas make superb bedding; equally they are good specimen plants; and they also mix well with other genera.

Floribundas or Cluster-Flowered Roses

It was also deemed necessary to change the name of these roses from 'Floribunda' to 'Cluster Flowered'. This met with similar resistance, and it is now common to find both titles used simultaneously. Floribunda rolls off the tongue much more easily than the cumbersome alternative, and is the one I continue to use. As their name suggests, these roses flower abundantly for a long season. They are relaxed in growth, compared with the Hybrid Teas, with loosely formed flowers borne in trusses, providing bountiful colour in a kaleidoscope range. Highly scented Floribundas are in the minority, but as they are chosen more for colour this is not a vital requirement. Their use in the garden is diverse. They make excellent bedding roses, providing long seasons of massed flower. Taller cultivars make good hedges, whilst shorter ones can be used to edge paths and driveways. Floribundas can be grown in tubs and some of the strong-stemmed varieties are useful to flower arrangers.

Miniature and Patio Roses

Miniature roses are indeed tiny versions of the Floribunda. Patio roses are less easy to distinguish, and were perhaps given this title for marketing purposes. Catalogues often list them separately, but there are other roses just as much at home in pots on the patio; equally, patio roses can be grown elsewhere.

Miniature and patio roses: 'Sweet Dreams'

Climbing and Rambling Roses

What is the difference between a climber and a rambler? This is a frequently asked question. The simple answer would be that climbers climb and ramblers ramble, which is largely true and probably enough to guide most gardeners when choosing varieties. There are, however, more precise differences. Climbers flower on growth produced earlier in the year whereas ramblers flower on the growth made the previous year. Many climbers flower repeatedly or continuously throughout the summer, whilst ramblers have just one flush, often followed by hips. Generally speaking, climbers are more suited to growing on pillars, against trellis or walls; ramblers, being more vigorous, cope with such demanding tasks as growing into trees or over unsightly buildings. In both cases, it takes up to two or three years before they begin to look established, and sometimes this long before the very vigorous ramblers start to flower.

Climbers

Climbing Bourbons

As with their shorter kin, they flower abundantly and are highly perfumed. The famous variety 'Zéphirine Drouhin' is found here; the cerise pink and generously perfumed flowers go on and on, but the biggest asset to this rose is that it is completely thornless, as is its sport 'Kathleen Harrop'. They are ideal candidates for gardens for the blind or in situations frequented by children. If the Climbing Bourbons can be faulted, it is for a tendency to mildew later in the season. Grow in open, airy situations, which are not too dry.

Climbing Bourbons: 'Zéphirine Drouhin'

Climbing Hybrid Teas

The majority of these roses are sports of the bush Hybrid Teas and therefore have large flowers in a range of colours. Unlike their shorter counterparts, however, none flower continuously, giving instead a repeat flush in early autumn. A tendency to grow in an upright manner requires training to prevent them from being top heavy, but otherwise they make excellent climbers.

Climbing Hybrid Teas: 'Ophelia'

Climbing Floribundas: 'Iceberg'

Climbing Floribundas

As with the Hybrid Teas, the climbing versions of the Floribunda are sports from the bush roses of the same variety. They are less prone to upright, top-heavy growth, and produce large clusters of flowers once or twice a year. Amongst their ranks are some well known, excellent climbers.

Modern Climbers

Rather like Modern Shrubs, these roses have such complicated parentage that they cannot be placed easily in any other classification, and so have ended up in one large group. The majority are free flowering and a large number scented, but because of their individual lineage they each have distinct characteristics. Perhaps because breeders have exercised their right to play with the genealogy of these roses, nearly all

are merit worthy, with some superior qualities, be it perfume, strength or beauty of flower. Within this group there must be at least one to match the best in all the other families of climbing roses.

Noisettes

Some very beautiful roses are in this group. Noisettes possess freedom of flower (in fact they were among the first to give perpetual blooming) with graceful growth and delicate perfumes. They are the connoisseur's climbing roses, not brash or overcoming, just perfectly natural. Although some are not totally hardy and need careful placing, there are varieties that will put up with almost anything, 'Mme. Alfred Carrière' being the prime example. This rose can cope with shade and poor soil, even a north wall, and will still produce sumptuous cupped blooms of porcelain cream, tinged with blush, with a super fragrance. 'Mme. Alfred Carrière' is of the most popular climbing roses at our nursery, proof that a good rose has a long life, having been introduced in the UK for the first time in 1879.

Climbing Teas

Not a very large group and certainly not the hardiest of roses, the Climbing Tea rose needs careful placing in a spot protecting it against winter weather. If this can be found, they are among the most exquisite climbers, possessing beauty and perfume that will pervade the warm summer air. If such a site is not possible, they will grow well in the greenhouse or cool conservatory. Many have been lost over the years, probably because of their less-than-strong disposition.

Ramblers

The Arvensis Hybrids

Native to Europe, Rosa arvensis, 'The Field Rose', is still often seen growing in the hedgerows of Britain, demonstrating just how hardy this group is. Also often called the Ayrshires, they are a small group of ramblers and scramblers in shades of white or pink. They often have purple shoots and dark leaves, a lovely backdrop to the flowers, which appear in abundance in mid-summer. Not heavily perfumed and not always hugely proportioned, this useful selection of roses has the advantage of growing happily almost anywhere.

The Boursaults

This is a very small, but interesting, group of medium-sized ramblers. No one is really sure how the Boursaults came about, long-standing theories of a rela-tionship with the China roses recently being dispelled thanks to the wonders of science. The Boursaults are not for the colder climates where they would suffer, but are fairly hardy elsewhere. Thornless branches are adorned with attractive foliage on tidy plants. The flowers, in shades of pink to magenta, are not huge in proportion and are often of a ragged style, but are none the less attractive.

Moschata Hybrids

Rosa moschata has been around since the reign of Henry VIII, and has given us a long line of descendants, both direct and indirect, including the Hybrid Musks, Noisettes, and via them the Floribundas. The Moschatas themselves are usually distinguishable by their grey-green leaves which are slender and tend to

droop. An advantage is that they tend to flower much later than other ramblers, usually in July, so that, by mixing them with other ramblers, a longer season can be achieved. Most bear small flowers, usually gently scented.

The Arvensis Hybrids: 'Düsterlohe'

The Boursaults: 'Morlettii'

Multiflora Ramblers

The Multifloras are vigorous, and in some examples capable of reaching a considerable height; this makes some of them ideal candidates for climbing into trees. Roses blooming through the branches of trees can be a spectacle in mid-summer, and some really will get to the top of mature trees by fighting their way through the branches towards the light. It's worth looking out for some of the smaller, more hybrid varieties, such as 'Narrow Water' and 'Phyllis Bide', that flower continuously well into the autumn, or for some of the more unusual purple-toned ones such as 'Violette', which will provide a contrast to the softer-coloured ramblers.

Sempervirens Hybrids

For the most part introduced in Victorian times, this is a most useful little group of ramblers, for they remain evergreen in all but the most severe winters. They are good subjects for arches and pergolas because they are so dense in growth, but also give good displays if grown elsewhere. Large clusters of flowers, in pastel shades, some of them little pompons, almost obliterate the foliage in mid-summer. They are healthy, vigorous and easy to grow.

Wichuraianas

In this group are some of my favourite ramblers. Rosa wichuraiana itself, with masses of small white, single flowers, is best used as a large procumbent, although it will ramble or scramble through hedgerows; contrariwise I have seen one or two of the ramblers used to cover banks, where they are extremely effective. One or two of the Wichuraianas break the once-flowering rule, flowering continuously well into the autumn; 'New Dawn' is perhaps the best known for this, and 'Gardenia' (which has a heavenly citrus-like perfume) will often give an extra few flowers later on. 'Dorothy Perkins' and 'Albertine' are two of the best-known cottage-garden roses, but are sadly prone to mildew after flowering; they do demonstrate, however, the two distinct styles of flowers found in this group: clusters of small pompons and larger more blowsy blooms. Ignoring those with a tendency to mildew, the Wichuraianas are largely healthy and versatile roses. They grow on pergolas and archways very effectively but also work well against the wall or trellis, or on pillars.

Sempervirens Hybrids: 'Félicité Perpétue'

Standard Roses

The nodding bows of a Weeping Standard.

Standard roses are simply varieties budded on to a host stem at specific heights. They have many uses in the garden, from working as a centrepiece in a rose bed, to growing in pots on the patio. The essential element of the Standard rose is height; by growing them in pots they become moveable features, which can be placed as a focal point anywhere. Although planting and training is discussed later, (*see* p. 58), it is essential to stress that all Standards must be well staked. The branches of a shrub Standard will become heavy, and can cause the stem to snap if not supported.

Modern Standards

These are budded at 3ft 6in (1m). By the time the rose at the top is established, they will be in the region of 5ft (1.5m). Different growers choose some of their most popular suitable varieties to bud as Standards and many different varieties of Hybrid Tea and Floribunda are available. Bearing in mind that they will flower at eye level, it is wise to ensure that the chosen variety is healthy: diseases will be much more obvious.

Shrub Standards

Once again, these are budded at 3ft 6in (1m), but they will become taller than their modern counterparts. Growers select continuous-flowering and often perfumed varieties, and a wide range is available. One of the best Shrub Standards is 'Bonica', which will flower over and over again on a very tidy plant.

Weeping Standards

Weeping Standards make fantastic features in the garden. They are propagated to be taller than the others, to allow the cascading branches further to tumble whilst maintaining the height of the overall plant. Rambling roses are usually used for this purpose and require training, (*see* Chapter Four for advice).

Standard Roses are dominant garden features.

Roses can be grown practically anywhere in the garden, from hanging baskets and window boxes to wooded areas and open parkland. They can happily climb through the branches of the tallest of trees or sprawl across the ground. They can also be practical if used to hide eyesores or create barriers. Wherever they are grown, roses can be the most beautiful of garden plants and no matter how small or difficult a garden may be, there is always a place for a rose.

Garden Design

2

Designing with roses

Large leaves of companion
plants provide contrast.

Roses in mixed planting

Whilst roses make fantastic flowerbeds
on their own, they can look equally wonderful mixed with other plants. In fact,
whether they are in the majority in any
scheme or just used occasionally, they
will naturally enhance companion plants
which in turn compliment them.

Cottage-style gardens do this wonderfully, usually using old-fashioned
varieties of shrub, climbing and herba-
ceous plants, such as lilac, foxgloves,
lupins and clematis in a soft palette of
colour from white and blush-pink
through to lavender and muted purples.
In amongst these are roses from the
same colour scheme, but contrasting
with immediately neighbouring plants.
Pillars, walls and arches are adorned
with honeysuckle, clematis and wisteria,
cleverly mixed with climbing and rambling roses of a different flowering
period. The overall effect is a harmony of
different shapes and gentle colours.

Of course a mixed bed or border
does not have to follow any particular
style. It can consist of plants that simply
appeal, planted according to size and
flowering. Unless it is to be a seasonal
scheme, care should be taken to mix
plants with different flowering times to
extend the colour for as long a period as
necessary; include evergreen shrubs and
bulbs as well for the winter and spring.
Whilst most roses have a continuous or
repeating period of bloom, those that
just flower once generally do so in such
abundance that this makes them ideal
candidates for mingling amongst other
plants with different seasons. Standard
roses and pillars or obelisks covered with
smaller climbing and rambling varieties
add height; the inclusion of spring flowering bulbs, evergreens and winter-flow-
ering and winter-fruiting plants (many
roses set hips) further prolongs the eye-
catching display.

A bed of roses

The bed or border can be of roses alone, either a variety of different ones, all the same or a few planted in a repeating pattern. If there is to be a range of varieties, size must be addressed. Shrub roses in particular come in a selection of shapes and sizes. Taller varieties should be placed towards the back of the border or in the centre of the bed; if it is wide enough, an almost tiered effect can be achieved by gradually using shorter varieties until the edge is reached.

A border of old-fashioned shrub roses is best when of mixed varieties; they compliment each other charmingly and the naturally fluid growth style found with so many of them allows them to mingle well. The Bourbons, Gallicas, Hybrid Perpetuals and Portlands make a good combination, as do the Hybrid Musks, Older Floribundas, Polyanthas, and some of the Teas and Chinas. Pimpinellifolias, Rugosas, Species, Centifolias and some of the larger Modern Shrubs such as 'Cerise Bouquet' can be more difficult to place because of their individual habits of growth; they are probably better employed in the mixed shrubbery, as hedging or with roses of their own kind. Restricting the selection to one family can also be successful, as they will share similar habits.

Whilst beds and borders are a definite feature of roses, it is nice to see them finished off with edging. This can be done using an unbroken chain of identical dwarf roses or other plants such as lavender, box or catmint; or a more structured edge can be formed from brickwork or wood. Corrugated plastic strips can be purchased specifically to define such margins, but I find these incongruous and less practical than the other choices. Low planting at the front serves several purposes: it edges the bed; it conceals weeds when there just isn't time to remove them; and, should any of the roses become leggy through lack of pruning or being nibbled by rabbits, it hides this also.

If a simpler, yet equally stunning, scheme is required, beds and borders can be of one singular variety. In a formal modern rose garden this is often the case and works so effectively. The beauty of beds and borders of particular varieties is that every rose will bloom at the same time giving a truly mass display. Conversely, the drawback is that they will all die off at the same time, leaving an unattractive sea of dead flowers.

A rose border of mixed
varieties in pastel shades.

Growing roses *en-masse* can produce enchanting
results whether mingled in together or planted in a
more structured manner.

The rose garden

True devotees may wish to have the major part of their garden full of roses or in a large garden an area may be designated solely for the purpose of growing roses. A rose garden does not have to exclude other plants, nor should it, but they are best employed to compliment the roses without dominating them. Companion plants bring different textures and flowering seasons to the garden as well as adding a broader range of colour, such as blue, which does not yet exist among roses. The roses are, however, the important features, and much forethought should be applied before planting can commence.

There are no set rules as to the design of rose gardens. New ideas or different concepts on old ones come along all the time and, as with everything, the choice should be totally personal. Broadly speaking, they fall into two categories: formal and informal.

Formal rose gardens

A formal rose garden is comprised of clearly designed beds and borders, and may be, as in the case of many old rose gardens, especially those of the Edwardian era, totally symmetrical, each half or even quarter reflecting the rest. This is shown in the specimen plan of a rose garden here: the varieties used are a mirror image in each quarter. This theory can be taken further into the creation of 'knot'-style gardens, where the beds are more intricately shaped or made simpler by using only two beds. Two long beds with a water feature running between them looks particularly stunning, the beds being a mirror image of each other with the colour of the roses reflected in the water.

Another approach is to have large circular beds (or other strong, definite shapes), each filled with a particular variety. A Standard rose can be included to give the bed some height. These beds are often cut from an established lawn, but the pathways between the beds need not be grass; shingle, wooden decking, bark, brick-weave or any other appropriate material can also be used.

It is often the case in large gardens that the rose area is partitioned from the whole, sometimes with trellis adorned with roses, with walls or with hedges. Rose gardens such as these have a magical ambience, for within their confines they become a personal and private place. When it is not possible to create this in a small garden, it is truly worth finding a public one to enjoy.

A formal garden is often symmetrical with central features.

Informal rose gardens

Informal gardens are usually designed more randomly with fewer geometrically styled beds. Crescent- and half-moon-shaped beds are found; there are fewer straight edges, and more natural curves; and there is very little symmetry. The balance usually varies throughout the garden, some areas concentrating on low-growing, procumbent roses, whilst others feature taller shrub roses and modern bedding roses. Garden ornaments and other embellishments are easy to situate when the garden is designed in a casual way. A bench or swing-seat should be included so the roses can be enjoyed as well as tended. Statues, bird-baths and tubs can be strategically positioned to be discovered mingling among the roses without the onlooker's prior awareness of them. Supportive structures such as obelisks and pillars allow the inclusion of climbers and ramblers, whilst procumbent roses tumble down the sides of urns, chimney-pots or other tall containers, providing a means of adding controlled height.

The Scented Garden

Roses are one of the most obvious candidates for the scented garden. Do, however, use your own nose to pick out varieties; one person may believe a rose possesses a wonderful perfume, whilst another may find it completely devoid of any. A scented garden for the blind is more difficult to create from roses because of their thorns, but there are some worth including. 'Zéphirine Drouhin' and 'Kathleen Harrop', both old Bourbon climbers, are completely thornless and considered by most to be heavily perfumed.

A less formal rose garden.

Climbers and ramblers

Climbing and rambling roses are a spectacle when in full flush, but they do need support in one way or another, unless it is the intention that they should just spill across the ground. If climbers and ramblers are desired in the garden, it is likely that there are places to grow them without the necessity or expense of purpose-built structures. The walls of the house are the first and most obvious props, but care must be taken when selecting roses for a northerly aspect (*see* Chapter Nine for some suggested varieties), as only the most hardy will be happy there. Eyesores such as oil tanks and scruffy outbuildings can be easily camouflaged under a veil of roses, similarly disused telegraph poles and gateposts. Ramblers will happily scramble through hedgerows and can be used effectively for filling gaps where the hedge has become a little thin; it must be remembered however, that trimming should take place after flowering and reduces the number of hips if the variety used sets them.

Try growing ramblers into trees. There are few more glamourous sights than a dark, foliated tree festooned with the tumbling clusters of flowers from a vigorous rambling rose. Remember, though, that a tree uses most of the nutrients and water that is also required by the rose, necessitating good husbandry in the early growing years and extra organic material at the time of planting. Be prepared for back-breaking digging when preparing the hole, for established trees have incredible root systems. Once a rambler starts to grow through a tree, provided it is given a good start, it will penetrate through the branches quickly to find the light.

Roses for the balcony

If a balcony is the only outdoor area, some roses can grow in hanging baskets or window boxes. They will not take a rose of huge proportions because there just isn't enough root space, so any variety that is too large would become stunted and probably not flower very well. Good examples to use are cultivars from the Procumbent group, that pendulously cascade down from the container, or some of the Polyanthas and low-growing Floribundas, which are more upright but still quite dainty. Miniature roses are not ideal in hanging baskets as their growth is too upright, but planted in twos or threes they can work well in window boxes. It is very important that both hanging baskets and window boxes are planted correctly (*see* Chapter Four for how to do this).

Miniature roses will grow happily in window boxes and look splendid when underplanted with bedding or trailing perennials.

Roses for the patio

On the patio, or strategically placed over manhole covers and other locations where there is no root space, roses both look splendid and perform well in tubs or containers of bigger proportion to the window box. Provided there is a good supply of nutrients in the form of a good compost and adequate drainage, coupled with the discipline of feeding and regular watering, even a Rambler can excel. It is unlikely to reach the same heights as its counterpart in the garden, simply because its roots do not have the same area to occupy, but this is not detrimental to overall performance. Any rose can be grown in a container, from chimneypot to magnificent urn, but the larger the rose the larger the container should be in order to achieve full potential. A half barrel (full-sized) would be appropriate for a vigorous climber or rambler, whilst a bucket-sized tub or chimneypot is more suited to the smaller shrubs. There are various types of pot made from all manner of materials, from plastic to marble; choose the pot to compliment the garden first, then choose the rose to grow in it. A rose grown in a tub is convenient because it can be positioned anywhere; it can even be moved around; it is also rewarding because it is more demanding of time and skill than a rose growing in the ground.

Concealing tree stumps

Tree stumps can be difficult to remove and difficult to cope with in the garden. There are two ways of overcoming this problem with roses, depending on the size of the stump. If the stump is tall, simply cover it in sprawling Ramblers; if it is short, hollow it out and plant a rose in it. Ensure that some drainage holes are drilled in low down and that drainage is assisted with the addition of rubble or shingle. A soil-based compost is best; after a few years it will not even need watering as the roots penetrate into the soil below. 'Bonica' looks fabulous when grown in this manner, as do most of the Procumbent group.

Roses look good in pots and tubs and have the added advantage of being portable.

Creating height

Giving height in the garden in places where there is no physical structure to support roses, provides an opportunity to be artistically creative, even original. In modern gardens try picking up something from the scrapyard. It doesn't matter what it is, provided it can be secured safely, will not tumble down after a short period and is large and strong enough to take the height and weight of a rose. Parts of children's garden toys, swings and climbing-frames may be found lurking in the corner of the garden of a home where children have since grown up, and they make ideal supports for roses. If something more conventional appeals, pillars of roses are simple to create using rustic poles easily obtained from a garden centre, but do ensure they are treated before situating them. Rope or chain swags can be hung between poles, with the climbing or rambling roses trained along them; this was a popular way of growing roses in 19th-century France, and is both elegant and practical. Swags of roses can be used to frame areas of the garden or to line pathways creating a boundary that does not entirely obstruct the view beyond.

An obelisk combines man made formality and the natural informal growth of the rose growing against it.

Obelisks

Obelisks are available in anything from wood to plastic-coated metals, and have the advantage of providing more width than the conventional pole. They are ideal for training the smaller ramblers which can be spiralled around them, difficult to achieve on a pole. Obelisks, trellis and pillars are available from mail-order suppliers, with a container attached at the base; this allows climbing or roses to be placed almost anywhere, even on the patio. Archways can also be found in this style, and, although none of these structures is easy to move, they do provide scope for use as mobile features for placing in prominent places when they are at their best.

Pergolas

If space allows, one of the most beautiful features is a pergola. This is basically a tunnel created from roses supported on a wooden or metal framework. To be practical, it can be situated over existing pathways with a definite destination, or be included in the garden as a dividing boundary disguising the vegetable patch or play area perhaps, or simply because a pergola is a beautiful, desirable feature. It should be wide enough to allow two people to walk through side by side and tall enough to accommodate a few tumbling blooms without obstructing headroom. Designs vary, but one of the most popular is a series of steel hoops, placed at equal distances with swags between each. A rustic pergola can be made quite easily from wooden poles placed equidistantly in two lines. Further poles are placed across and between each one at the top. If desired, more can be attached on each side, either at the same or varying heights and the roses can be trained around them to create windows to the garden beyond. How the roses are used is up to you. Tradition would dictate that the same variety is used in opposite positions, thus achieving equal growth and bands of colour, but there is no reason, other than formality, why they cannot be mixed. Ramblers are usually more stunning on a pergola than climbers, but I prefer to see a mixture of both to provide continuity of flower. With training they can be intermingled so there is a complete covering, and the bands of colour are less defined.

Gazebos and arbours are stunning focal points and the ideal places to take shelter from mid-summer sun and enjoy the roses.

Gazebos and arbours

Gazebos and arbours are a lovely setting for drinks on a summer's evening, and as such should be adorned with gloriously scented roses. A gazebo is rather like a summerhouse, but its construction is open, with trellis often used for panelling, and has wide entrances. A traditional design is hexagonal in shape with a pointed roof, but they can be circular or squared. Often large enough to accommodate a table and chairs, a gazebo should be placed where it is a focal point, as well as where views across the garden can be enjoyed. Whilst usually built from wood, some manufacturers of garden ornamentation retail the complete or self-assembly structures made in galvanised steel or plastic-coated metals imitating wrought iron. Arbours are also available in similar fabrics, or can be easily homemade, with an arch-like construction, filled in on one of the open sides and a bench placed within. Arbours should be carefully placed to take full advantage of the view of the garden in a hospitable sheltered area perhaps in one corner, beneath a tree or against a wall.

Fences

Plain timber fences with two or three horizontal rails can be much enhanced by rambling or climbing roses and make a good framework to train them against. The roses not only look wonderful as part of the boundary, but also have the advantage that their thorny disposition acts as extra security as well. Arching branches can easily be tied in to encourage lateral growth from which the roses will flower freely.

Roses make excellent flowering boundaries and because most are thorny they also act as intruder deterrents.

The rose hedge

Leylandii, beech, privet and other evergreen shrubs are often seen used as hedging, not so often the rose; however, rose hedges should be more common-place. The best roses to use as hedging are the Rugosas, and they have much going for them over other hedging plants. Rugosas flower; are scented; have dense growth; set fantastic hips; have autumn colour; and are very thorny – few intruders would want to fight their way through a vicious barrier such as a Rugosa hedge. They are also very tough, and generally disease resistant. More than one variety of the Rugosas can be grown together successfully to provide maximum interest. Colours vary from white to the deeper pink hues, and all those in this range work well together. But if you want the hips, avoid the few of those in the yellow spectrum which barely ever fruit.

Most of the Rugosa are of medium size, usually around 5ft (1.2m). A shorter hedge can be easily achieved using some of the older roses; the Portlands such as 'Comte de Chambord' will happily arrive at 3ft (1m) and are unlikely to get much taller than that. The smaller Centifolias, too, remain around that size, and the modern Hybrid Teas and Floribundas make neat and tidy hedging. For larger boundaries, many of the Species roses come into their own, but they do need the space to spread and will sprawl more than the Rugosas.

Roses by the water's edge

Reflections of roses in rippling water and the gentle trickle of a stream or splashing of a fountain: what could be nicer? This is easy to achieve – provided the land around is not too wet. With formal garden ponds, plant roses around part of the edge, but not too close if the pond is made from a fabric or plastic liner because the roots might penetrate through. Choose naturally lax varieties like 'The Fairy', whose small pompon flowers hang in trusses, or if the pond is larger, then some of the Hybrid Musks are appropriate.

If the water is already part of the landscaped garden, a brook for instance, much larger varieties can be selected. The Centifolias, some of the larger Gallicas and roses such as the Pimpinellifolia 'Frühlingsduft' and the shrub rose 'Cerise Bouquet' all work well by the water because they are graceful and curvaceous. If these are too big, some of the Bourbons will fit the bill. If there is a bridge in place, try growing Ramblers on to it, one on each side from each end so that there is still some rail to hold on to.

Species roses should in my opinion compliment a natural water feature, especially if the surrounding area has not been landscaped. Rosa arvensis 'The Field Rose', is wonderful at the water's edge, as are some of the ramblers which will beautifully trail down the banks of the river or lakeside.

The blooms of this rambler are beautifully reflected in the still water.

A natural setting

Places such as woodland, countryside parkland and the wild or conservation areas tend not to be so much gardened, as just tidied occasionally, so roses that thrive on neglect are the best choices for these places. Species and the more gangly hardy hybrids will naturally consort with the wilder area, and after a while look as though they have always belonged there. Planting a rambler without support often produces good results: it will tumble over in a fountain-like manner, which is relaxed and unarranged. In open parkland, plant roses as specimen plants and leave them to do their own thing. It will not matter if they fall to one side or grow across the ground; this is what they would do naturally. For the conservation garden, select roses with perfume to attract insects and hips for the birds, but if rabbits are present put some form of protection around the young plant to prevent succulent shoots from being nibbled.

Roses in the greenhouse

As a child, I remember plants of the older Hybrid Teas growing on pillars in my father's greenhouses. One in particular was the variety 'Uncle Walter', with its voluptuous, scented red blooms, which appeared earlier than other roses growing outside and were ideal cut flowers. But few people are lucky enough to have substantial greenhouses in which to grow roses all year round. However, even a small structure may have just enough room for one or two roses or just be used for over-wintering the more tender varieties. The Teas and the Chinas are the obvious choices; whether brought in for the winter months or grown inside all the time, they are less hardy than most and are extremely rewarding under glass. Extra heat is not necessary, in fact they need no more attention than roses grown in tubs outdoors, except perhaps needing a little more water. If space allows, the climbers amongst them can be trained on wires placed about 1ft (0.3m) away from the glass where they will supply shade for lower-growing plants in high summer.

The hedge and arch-way encourage the eye to the statue beyond.

Choosing the right roses can be a difficult and complicated decision because so many are available. A trip to a garden centre to see what looks nice is not recommended, because you can never be really sure whether the rose will adapt to the particular situation intended for it. The best approach is to plan requirements before looking.

Choosing, Buying and Planting

Deciding on the right rose

Rose breeders continually strive to produce the perfect rose, but perfection to
one gardener may mean something
quite different to another, so it is likely
that many of the varieties considered will
not entirely fit the desired requirements.
First, choose your priorities. Probably
there is not one variety of rose that:
flowers all summer long; is wonderfully
perfumed; is totally disease resistant; will
never need pruning; and is available in
the colour or style needed. So a list of
priorities is helpful.

Once the necessities have been
determined, consideration can be given
to the varieties needed. Chapter One,
The Various Family Groups, can help
define which family group is a practical
choice. Chapter Eight, *Roses for
Particular Situations*, suggests roses
that are ideal for difficult places, but
this is still not the complete picture.

Nurseries

There can be no substitute for visiting
rose gardens and nurseries to view roses
for oneself. Taste is a very personal thing
and no one can really describe a rose
fully, no matter how many words they
use. When it comes to scent appreciation
what one may consider a strong perfume, another may struggle to detect.

Flower shows

Visiting a flower show is another way to
view roses, but do remember that the
grower may be displaying cut blooms
rather than whole plants, and that,
especially early in the summer, the roses
may have been forced into flower under
glass, hence appearing a little less lush
in colour than usual.

Making a selection

Having seen the roses you like in reality,
or if you are selecting them out of season, rose encyclopedias and specialist
catalogues (advertised in the classified
sections of gardening magazines) contain a wealth of information, and are one
of the most valuable aids in choosing the
best varieties. They give accurate size
guides and tell you what a particular cultivar will tolerate; there are roses that will
cope with poor soil, shade or even worse
situations if necessary but many that will
not (*see* Chapter Eight).

Roses are available in pots
pre-packed from shops,
garden centres and mail order.

Bare root roses are freshly dug from the fields.

The Nurseryman ties up bundles of roses in the field to make it easier to handle large quantities.

Bare root roses

Roses are available for purchase in different forms and from varying suppliers. Pre-packed, bare-root plants can be found in a variety of places, including supermarkets and market stalls, during the autumn and winter months. Bearing a cardboard label, usually featuring a photograph of neatly arranged and over-sized blooms, they will have been packed in a polythene bag with a little damp peat around the roots to stop them drying out. I would not recommend buying a rose packed this way. The damp peat is conducive to disease, and, if stored indoors, the heat created by the packaging tricks the rose into growth; after a while, if not purchased, the peat dries out and the tender shoots and young roots that have developed die back – not a good start. Such a rose requires very heavy pruning and soaking in order to reinstate any vitality.

Many garden centres also sell pre-packed bare-root roses, but these will generally have just the roots wrapped in a little compost and polythene. This allows inspection of the stems; if they appear wrinkled, it is likely that the rose has dried out at some point; it should be left on the shelf. Garden centres and non-specialist nurseries are preferable to supermarkets, but be aware that the choice may be limited.

The most successful source is almost certainly ordering bare-root roses direct from the specialist nurseries that grow them; they provide the complete service, and, because they are mail order, all the purchasing can be done from the luxury of your armchair.

The roses are then laid out in their sorts ready to be picked to compile customer's orders.

Request several catalogues, before deciding which growers to deal with. Prices will be found to vary, but a higher price does not reflect superior quality – perhaps the various factors connected with the cost of production and the royalties required by the breeders of specific varieties. Also, new roses are often more expensive, reflecting the cost of introducing them to the market place. The catalogues describe the roses on offer in enough detail to aid selection, but a good supplier is happy to lend their expertise over the phone, should their collection prove to be overwhelming.

Place the order in the summer months, and in autumn or winter the roses will arrive in their dormant state ready for planting; the period between can be spent improving the ground into which they are to be planted.

Containerized roses

Containerized roses are also readily available from different sources; however, the choice may not be as wide ranging as in the specialist catalogues, and it is unlikely that they will be delivered to you. The largest selections are found at the nurseries of the specialists, but garden centres that have purchased them from wholesalers, also stock them. Occasionally roses in containers are found in high-street stores, but careful scrutiny should be given to their quality before purchase. Container roses are becoming more popular because they meet the demands of those wanting to create instant gardens; also they can be obtained in spring and summer when bare-root roses are not available. Container roses are from the same stock

A strong bare root rose will have several well spread branches and a good root system The specimen below, by comparison only has couple of spindly branches and a very poor root system.

as the bare-root roses of the previous winter, having been placed in a pot for this convenience. They will also remain in the pot for a long period, if the planting place cannot be made ready, and must be watered regularly. One of the advantages of buying roses in this way is that you can see what you are buying; both the nature of the flower and the quality of the plant can be ascertained.

Selecting a good specimen

The size of a rose plant depends largely on the typ of rose you are buying, and the older roses vary co siderably. The Teas and Chinas, and a few of the o old-fashioned roses, are likely to produce more flimsy growth with less branches, so be sure to all for this when selecting them. The more modern a stronger-growing varieties have more rigid and thicker growth. With the exceptions mentioned, ne roses should have at least three, preferably more, main stems originating at the base. Procumbent roses and some ramblers may have an array of smaller slightly contorted stems. If roses are being supplied by post from a reputable grower, you can be reasonably sure that: the plants are of a good quality; have been well looked after before despatch; and have been carefully prepared for their journey. If, when they arrive, you are in doubt as to the condition of any of them, notify the nursery; most growers guarantee their roses for a defined period and replace failures, but are happier doing so if they are made aware of the problem sooner rather than later.

Pests and diseases

As well as its size and shape, a containerized rose should be examined for signs of damage or disease before taking it home. Most growers, unless intentionally organic, operate a spraying regime, which should prevent disease problems; it is worth checking to be sure. A few aphids are often inevitable in mid-summer and should not put you off buying a rose; they can be dealt with later.

Containerized roses

All roses in containers should be well labelled. There is nothing worse than buying a selection, only to find when you get them home that you do not know which is which. Climbing roses in containers should be supported by a cane, which assists in transporting them without breakage. Standard roses should have at least three main branches originating at the stem, but if there is no possibility of purchasing such a good one

(their numbers are often limited), it may be possible to train it into shape with careful pruning later on. Check that the stem is not damaged, and, if containerized, that it has a support of some description already in place. If suckers are found on the stem or emerging from the pot, ask the grower to remove them. They are a natural occurrence that cannot be avoided, especially when the stem is young; by watching the nurseryman remove them you will learn the most effective way of doing so.

Pre-packed roses

If a pre-packed rose is the only choice, try to discern that it is fresh. This is a difficult task, bearing in mind that the packaging prevents getting a good look at the whole plant. Feel the weight of it; peat that has become dry is very light, so if there is heaviness at the bottom it usually means that it is still moist. Wrinkles on stems also suggest that the rose has been allowed to dry out; if there is evidence of this, put it back. Try not to buy a pre-packed rose as spring approaches, or too early in the autumn, as the rose may not be fully dormant; in fact, milder temperatures may even encourage unnecessary growth whilst the rose is still in the packet.

planting roses

The arrival and heeling-in of bare-root roses

Bare-root roses that have been ordered for delivery may arrive any time in the autumn or winter. Commercial growers will have been accepting orders since the previous spring and may have many thousands to despatch. They do this on a rotational basis of first come first served, so an order placed early is most likely to be received in late autumn; one placed later may not be with its recipient until late winter or early spring.

When the order does arrive (usually by post), the roses will be found to be tied in bundles (a large number of roses can be compressed into quite a small bunch), and wrapped first in a strong polythene bag, then in a two- or three-ply paper bag. The roots will have been moistened before packing and, provided the parcel is left in a cool, frost-free place, the rose will not come to any harm if left for about a week when the weather is too bad for planting. If a week goes by and the weather still has not improved, the roses should be heeled-in in a temporary situation.

1 An area of ground should be prepared in advance by covering it with a thick piece of material such as carpet or hessian sacking to protect it from the frost.

2 Dig a trench with one side at an angle of approximately 45°.

3 Lay the roses evenly spaced but quite close together along the angled side; and replace the soil, making sure it is firmed in well. The roses can remain here for any length of time and will still be in good condition when it comes to planting them, but do plant them before they show any signs of growth in spring.

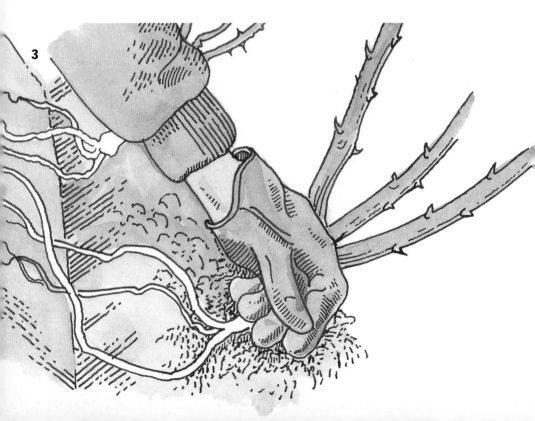

Planting bare-root roses

If you are planting more than one rose, into a bed for example, mark out the planting positions beforehand with canes, or, if these are not readily available, with sticks or large stones. Always dig a hole that is larger than the roots of the rose you are to plant and of similar shape. It should be deep enough to cover the union (the knobbly part of the rose where the stems and roots join) by at least an inch (2.5cm). Planting to this depth helps stabilize the plant, discourages suckers and ensures that all the roots are kept moist.

1 The hole should also be wide enough to enable gentle spreading of the roots; a plant with a wide root base is a more stable one.

2 A handful of bonemeal should then be thrown into the bottom of the hole and mixed into the soil here thoroughly with the spade, and then another handful should be combined into the soil that has been removed.

3 Trim any damaged or exceptionally long roots to the average length of the others.

4 Now place the rose in the centre of the hole, ensuring that the roots are well spread without force, and that it is upright; return enough of the soil into the hole to support it, using one hand to hold the plant and the other to return the soil.

5 Once it is standing freely in position, spade in about half of the soil; then gently shake the plant to ensure that every nook and cranny is accommodated.

6 Now return as much of the remaining soil as will fit; firm with the feet; and the last of the soil can then be added and neatened. Water the plant well and make sure that it is well labelled (the tag labels attached to most roses will begin to fade after a year or two).

Roses are usually potted into rigid, reusable plastic.

Planting a container rose

Follow all the guide-lines given above for planting a bare-root rose, but keep in mind the following points.

● Some authorities recommend that the roots of a container rose should be teased apart at planting time. I disagree with this if they are being planted during the summer. They will have developed many tiny, tender fibrous roots, which will be torn away if the root ball is disturbed; for this reason container roses need to be removed from their pot with care.

● Do not try to remove the rose from its container when it has been recently watered; the weight of the compost will be too much for the roots to support and it will fall away.

● If the rose is potted into a polythene-bag type of pot, removal is easily achieved by running a knife firstly around the base, then down the side, thus simply peeling the polythene away, but do take care not to penetrate the roots. However, this type of pot is not common today.

1 The pot is more likely to be made of rigid, reusable plastic. Do not try to cut through this with a knife; firstly, one slip could cause untold damage to the hand; and secondly, the pressure needed will almost certainly mean that the roots inside will be damaged. Instead, gently squeeze the pot to loosen the root ball from the edges.

2 With the base of the plant supported between two fingers, turn the pot upside down and further gently squeeze the pot until the entire contents come away in one piece. If this doesn't happen, enlist the help of the edge of a bench-top; simply tap the upper edge of the pot against it, whilst still supporting the rose upside down.

3 If the rose still refuses to leave the pot, a pair of strong scissors can be used to cut down the side, but this method should only be used as a last resort as it will render the pot unusable and the scissors blunted.

Planting techniques for container roses

● Be aware that when the nurseryman potted the rose, the roots may have been too large to allow the union to have been covered. If anything is above the level of the compost in the pot, other than branches, it should be buried at the time of planting, in order that the union is at least one inch (2.5cm) lower than ground level.

● As with the bare-root plant, care should be taken to dig the hole to the correct depth, and be sure that it is wide enough to firm around without disturbing the root ball. Mix in bonemeal as for the bare-root specimen, but remember that there will be some soil left over because of the mass of the root ball itself.

● Although they can be planted at any time, container roses are usually planted during the summer. The roots will have been restricted to grow in the confines of the pot in which they were purchased and it will take some time before they penetrate to more moist depths. They will, therefore, need soaking regularly after planting and for at least the remainder of the summer.

Planting roses into tubs

When choosing the container, bear in mind the ultimate size of the plant. Any rose, no matter how big, will grow in a small pot, if it is well cared for (although it may not reach full size), but it will look ridiculously unbalanced if it is in a pot inappropriate to its size. A multitude of containers is available, made from a variety of materials in all shapes and sizes.

A large rose needs a pot wide enough to keep it stable. Another point: a wooden tub can have its life extended if the sides are lined with plastic. Also, you could try growing roses in large plastic pots, so they can be moved later to a more elegant container.

1 Always assist drainage by placing shingle or stones in the base before adding a thin layer of organic matter.

2 Place a small amount of soil-based compost on top of this as it (retains nutrients better, does not dry out so quickly, and also weighs the pot down more successfully than a peat-based one) before going on to plant the rose using the same compost.

● Follow the suggestions above for planting bare-root and container roses depending which you have, ensuring that there is a gap of a couple of inches (5cm) between the soil level and the top of the pot to allow for watering.

● Every few years the rose will need to be re-potted. Do this in the dormant season when there is no risk of damaging new roots.

● Remove the rose from the container, retaining some compost around the roots but taking away the majority of it.

● Check that the drainage stones have not been removed during this process, and if necessary replace them; then repot the rose in the same way.

● Roses can also be planted in hollowed-out tree stumps. Line the sides with plastic, and if necessary bore a few drainage holes as close to the bottom of the stump as possible.

● Then plant as for any other container. Window boxes and hanging baskets should also have a layer of shingle near the base, but not too much, because they are more shallow and less likely to become water logged.

There are a number of whys and wherefores when it comes to pruning' which are given throughout this chapter. I do not wish to appear dictatorial in explaining them, so I begin within some good advice: be practical and use common sense. If you can't reach a branch and haven't got a stepladder, never mind; do it another time. If you feel a branch is just too thick for the strength you possess, leave it until a strong relation is visiting. You know that it's got to go, so you have won the major part of the battle; it will not deprive the plant that much if it's not taken away until next year. Above all don't be over-concerned, pruning and training are really quite simple tasks.

Pruning and Training

4

Pruning roses

There are three good reasons why roses are pruned:

● To encourage flowering; a plant containing a large amount of old wood, which is unlikely to manufacture bloom, struggles to support it as well as producing worthwhile flowers.

● To keep the plant within bounds and neat and tidy.

● To remove any damaged areas of growth that are open to possible infection. By pruning, the plants are rejuvenated: younger growth produces better foliage and flowers.

The essentials of pruning

There are many schools of thought when it comes to pruning. The more books and articles one reads, the more this becomes apparent. The ideas put forward by the various experts in the field are nearly always logical and have many similarities, but the best advice any gardener can take is: use common sense and look at the job in hand as the simple task it really is. Take one plant at a time and study it, before you start to determine if there is any damage to be removed, and to decide how it should look when it is finished. If in doubt about a particular branch, leave it; it can always be pruned next time or tidied when dead-heading.

Timing

Pruning is best carried out after the worst of the frosts have subsided during late winter/early spring. Some say it should be done in mid-winter, but I feel the risk of frost bite is too strong on open wounds. Besides, who wants to be outside pruning roses in the freezing cold when it can wait until the weather has improved?

Tools

Three important tools are required to prune successfully: **a pair of strong gardening gloves**, **good quality, sharp secateurs**, and **a pair of long-handled loppers** for removing thick branches and stumps. Strong-handed gardeners may find they can manage without the latter, but anyone like me will certainly need a pair. **A pruning saw** can also be helpful for very mature plants, and **a pair of florist's scissors** is useful for miniature roses. Some suggest that a kneeler is helpful, but I find pruning from such a position nigh on impossible. I prefer the freedom of being able to move around the plant as I work.

Principles of pruning

The golden rules of pruning are laid out below. If in reality they have to be broken, do not worry.

● Cuts should be made above an outward-facing bud; if the cut is made elsewhere, the stem will naturally die back to a node anyway.

● The cut should be at an angle sloping away from the bud to prevent rainwater becoming trapped here when the bud starts to grow.

● Cuts should be made as clean as possible.

● Always remove dead or badly diseased wood, which do nothing for the performance of the plant. When doing this, cut away all the damaged parts visible to the eye. Once the cut is made, it is possible to see the pith inside the stem; if this is white you have removed enough, but if some discoloured pith remains, cut away more.

● Always remove growth that has suffered damage through rubbing or being tied too tightly, as this is likely to die back or become diseased. At least one of two rubbing stems should be pruned back, even if there is no sign of damage now, the damage will occur later.

A hard pruned bush rose.

Pruning newly planted roses

All types of bare-root roses should be pruned very hard when they are first planted, leaving only three or four eyes on each stem. This is extremely important and is the foundation of a good plant, as it is the one opportunity to really encourage basal growth. A rose usually produces new growth from the top end of its branches; if the initial prune is not hard enough, the end result will be a top-heavy plant. Container roses will already have been pruned, at the right time, by the nursery that grew them, so they can be left unpruned at planting time; they will receive attention at the time of the annual prune.

Remove damaged wood where the tie has cut into the branch, as this is an ideal place for disease to enter.

Annual pruning of bush roses

Bush roses, in particular the modern Hybrid Teas and Floribundas, thrive if well pruned. Always remember that winter or spring pruning is the one annual overhaul the rose gets; in the case of these roses it is worth being thorough. Cut away any diseased, dead, dying and damaged wood before anything else; you can then see what you have left to prune and shape. Remove some of the central growth, as close to the base as possible, and any crossing branches; opening up a plant in this way promotes a good shape.

Each year remove one of the oldest branches: the rotation of always removing an old branch helps keep the plant young. This gives you the skeleton of the plant. Now reduce the branches that are left. Take thicker shoots back to about half their length and prune any thinner ones harder still; growth from them is willowy and weak. Don't forget that you should be cutting above an outward-facing bud, but if this is difficult to see, don't fret; any die-back will be concealed by leaves and can be snipped away on discovery later on.

In autumn it is advisable to cut bush roses back by about a third to prevent wind-rock. Their roots do not penetrate deeply, and if caught by the wind they will rock from side to side causing the soil around their base to move away. This open area in the ground quickly fills with rain and freezes in mid-winter, in turn freezing the rose.

1

Annual pruning of once-flowering shrub roses

Before giving the 'do's and don'ts' of pruning these roses, it is important to say that no rose gardener should be excessively worried about getting the pruning of them exactly right. They are very forgiving and may well perform excellently if pruning is missed. I would not advocate that they are never pruned. For one thing they would then take over, and for another they would be top heavy and misshapen, but the odd year over-looked is not going to do them that much harm. The roses you should not prune, other than the occasional tidy, are the Species roses, the Sweetbriars and most of the Pimpinellifolias. There are two reasons: firstly, most of these roses produce hips and a summer prune, dis-cussed below, destroys this occurrence; and secondly, they manage very well without pruning and are great charac-ters if left alone. Groups such as the Albas, Gallicas, Centifolias and Damasks flower on the previous year's growth and are best pruned when flowering has finished to allow them to produce wood on which to flower the next summer.

2

1 With the 'golden rules' in mind, start by cutting away any dead, diseased or damaged growth, and then remove any tangled central growth to let the light in. Cut away twiggy growth as it is unlikely to establish into anything worthwhile.

2 Then stand back to see exactly what you are left with.

3 Now all that is needed is a general tidy up; you do not want to destroy the plant's character. A summer prune should not be a hard prune, as that would cause the rose to lose moisture, which in turn slows down re-growth.

Pruning repeat-flowering shrub roses

The older Hybrid Teas, older Floribundas and Chinas should be treated in the same way as modern bush roses, described earlier (*see* p. 61). Rugosas should not be pruned very much at all, other than an occasional tidying or when they get out of control, in which case they will tolerate harsh treatment. If they are growing as a hedge, they can be lightly trimmed when the need arises. This is best done in spring rather than summer, so as not to impair hip-bearing ability. Tea roses require more gentle treatment; other than the removal of bad wood, they should just be tidied.

The Portlands, Hybrid Perpetuals, Bourbons and Hybrid Musks benefit from an annual prune to keep them rejuvenated and replenished with new flowering growth, and to prevent them from becoming top heavy and unsightly.

Portlands, Hybrid Perpetuals and Hybrid Musks benefit from an annual prune.

• To begin with, cut away any damaged, diseased or dead wood, ensuring that no affected parts of the stem are left. Then, as with the bush roses, take out some of the stems from the centre of the plant, cutting as close to the base as possible so as not to leave stumpy snags.

• Take away any spindly growth which is unlikely to be worthwhile to the plant and reduce a few main stems by about a third; these branches will give the plants their height.

• Reduce about half of the remaining branches to half their length and the rest to a third, in order to create a well-shaped plant.

• If there are any old stumps left at the base from previous year's pruning, remove them using a pair of longhandled loppers. You will now have the basis to begin a rotational system of pruning in future years.

• The branches that were left the longest this year can be the hardest pruned next time; they will not have had the chance to become too old and woody, and basal growth is encouraged in this way.

Training and supporting shrub roses

Most shrub roses by virtue of pruning manage to keep a good shape and do not require any training. Some, especially the larger Gallicas, Centifolias and Moss roses, and some of the Bourbons and Hybrid Perpetuals, have a tendency to produce long, arching growth which becomes weighed down when in flower. There are several methods by which these roses can be trained or supported to their benefit or to further enhance the design of the garden.

Using obelisks

Wide obelisks, made from wood or metal, provide a structure to twine the roses around. They can be placed over the rose, so that, with assistance, it grows up from within. The structure is still visible with the flowers appearing through the framework. The other way is to place the obelisk adjacent to the rose and train the branches around it. It is unlikely that you will be able to train the branches in a cork-screw fashion, as you would with a rambler, but by bending them around the structure as much as possible you encourage flowers along their length.

Using frames

A wooden framework can be built around the rose. Consisting simply of a square of wood with legs at each corner at around 2ft (0.6m) from the ground. Arching branches will fall against this and can be tied around it so that they do not all fall in the same direction, creating a fountain of colour.

Another way of achieving the same effect is to peg down the cascading stems, by using a metal peg at least 18in (46cm) long. The branch should be held by the peg towards its tip so that it is 1ft (0.3m) from the ground. There are two advantages of pegging down or using a frame: the first is that an individual rose can be encouraged to take up a large area; the other is that in training the stems out in this lateral way, flowering growth is encouraged, and there will probably be more flowers than if it were free standing.

Using pegs

Roses can be permanently pegged down, a method used a lot before the advent of Procumbent roses but one rarely seen now. When trained in this way, the plant is encouraged to grow to a much larger size than it would otherwise do. A hard prune should have been given at planting time to create maximum shoots. The plant is then not pruned; instead the branches are allowed to grow naturally until they are long enough to pull towards the ground without split-ting them, usually when they are two years old. They should then be held in place with long pegs 12in (30.5cm) from the ground. Snip away the end of the shoot, so that the length of it remains the same. From this shoot will grow many vertical flowering shoots, many more than would have been the case had the branch not been pegged in place. After flowering, or when pruning, these new branches can be cut back again or allowed to develop into long branches to replace or add to those already pegged.

Annual pruning and training of a climbing rose

As discussed earlier (*see* p. 35), there are distinct differences between the way Climbers and Ramblers grow and perform in the garden; it therefore follows that they should be treated in differing ways. In this section we are looking chiefly at the Noisettes, the climbing forms of Hybrid Teas, Bourbons, Hybrid Perpetuals, Teas and the group referred to as the Modern Climbers. All of these roses produce lateral stems that flower in the same season.

Training

The training of them is just as important as the pruning. If allowed to grow straight up, they will flower at the top leaving lower stems unclothed, so it is important that in all cases branches are trained as horizontally as possible. Stems can be bent over and secured against a support of some description, using plastic ties or soft garden string; do not use nylon string as this cuts into the flesh of the branch. On walls, the best support usually consists of a series of wires fixed in place horizontally.

Pruning

Climbers should always be hard pruned when they are planted. I have repeated this point several times, but it really must be stressed that a good plant is created by its first prune. During the first year it will produce strong climbing shoots which should be tied horizontally against the support, in a low position. From these new shoots will emerge. These flowering shoots should be reduced to about a third of their length at the next prune and once again tied horizontally. This process goes on until a blanket of branches is formed. The climber will then flower all over.

For Climbers growing on pillars or obelisks, the theory is much the same, but instead of bending the branches outwards they should be encouraged to grow around the structure rather than straight up it.

When pruning, keep an eye out for rubbing and damaged branches. By nature of the fact that they have many branches growing in a cris-cross fashion, this type of damage is likely to happen. Also check that string used to hold the branches in place is not becoming too tight and embedding itself. Any damage caused in this way should be removed.

Climbers and Ramblers are pruned in different ways.

Pruning and training rambling roses

As Ramblers – all the once-flowering groups – produce their flowering growth the year before, the way they are dealt with differs from the Climbers. Much of their new growth is made from the base, even on mature plants, so the method of training and pruning for low growth as used for the Climbers does not apply here. For this reason, if they are left unpruned it doesn't matter; in fact for their younger years it is best to leave them and after this they may only require attention every two to three years, or when they get out of control.

Pruning

Pruning that does take place should be done after flowering, so the plant has the opportunity of making new wood from which to flower the next summer. Take away one or two of the older stems at their base, using a pair of long-handled loppers. Make sure you are wearing a strong pair of gloves because these stems will have become entwined with others further up and it can be a prickly task to get them out. Remove any further stems, or parts of them, that are dead or diseased. Other than these, remove only stems that have flowered, but remember that in doing so you will loose autumn hips if the variety sets them. If the hips are a favourite feature, then either leave a few clusters of spent flowers, taking them off when the hips are decaying or have been eaten by birds, or leave the prune until the winter time on these specific plants. Some new growth will have been made and it is important to ensure that it remains, but a winter prune will mean fewer flowers later than on the summer-pruned or unpruned plant. A winter prune is however best reserved for very mature plants when more severe treatment is necessary, and is discussed later under Reviving Old Ramblers (*see* p. 73).

Training

When it comes to training, the long, arching branches should be encouraged outwards in the same way as the Climbers; from these the flowering shoots will appear. A rambler that is allowed to grow straight up will flower at the top, leaving bare branches below. Unless this is the intention, when growing a rambler into the branches of a tree for example, this should be discouraged.

Annual pruning and training of standard roses

As discussed in Chapter One (*see* p. 10), there are three main types of Standard rose, and the pruning method used depends on the type. As the flowering head of a Standard is merely a rose plant growing on and being nourished by a host stem, the pruning and training techniques are much the same as for the plant growing at ground level, with the exception of the Weeping Standards.

Probably the most awkward element of pruning a Standard rose in its early years is developing a good shape. A lop-sided Standard is much more noticeable than a bush rose and far less easy to disguise with companion planting.

Follow the guide-lines for pruning Hybrid Tea, Floribunda and Shrub roses found earlier in this chapter (*see* p. 64), and dead-head frequently, tidying as you go.

● Ensure that the stake is firmly in the ground and not rotting at the bottom. Check that the ties are not too tight.

● If any suckers have appeared at the base or on the stem, make sure that they are removed cleanly at their base.

Pruning and training a weeping standard

A Weeping Standard is a variety of rambling or climbing rose budded on to a host stem and most of the guide-lines to pruning are the same, except that the Standard version may need more frequent attention to training to ensure that they weep successfully.

Pruning

Once-flowering cultivars produce flowers on the growth they made the previous year. Therefore, they should be pruned after they have flowered, removing only wood that has produced blooms, stems that are rubbing against others, and any branches diseased or suffering from die-back.

● Leave the new growth - usually in the form of soft, pliable arching arms - for training and subsequent flowering the next summer.

● Repeat-flowering cultivars are given a light trim in the autumn and are more severely pruned in late winter/early spring. They also need regular dead-heading to perpetuate flowering.

● It does not matter if new growth is pruned; the most important factor to be aware of is shape.

● Keep the branches as open as possible, ensuring that dead, diseased and rubbing branches are dealt with.

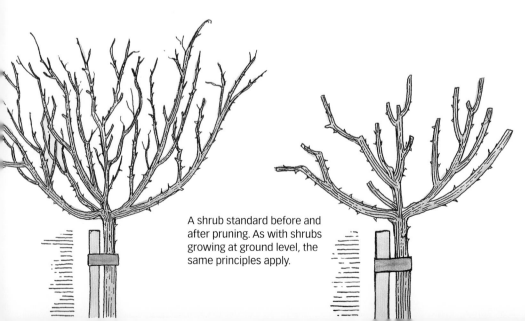

A shrub standard before and after pruning. As with shrubs growing at ground level, the same principles apply.

Training

Weeping Standards are taller than other types and have heavier heads. It is essential, therefore, to ensure that the stake is still strong and that the ties are still evenly spaced and are not perishing.

● The naturally arching branches of Weeping Standards need regular training to prevent ungainly growth.

● There are three ways of doing this. The first method is to purchase or make a training umbrella. This consists essentially of circles of wire, in the fashion of an upturned hanging basket. It is secured to the top of the stake (which must be left taller than the stem). As the branches grow, they can be tucked behind the wires to encourage them to grow in a weeping manner.

● A similar method is to use a single circular wire attached to two stakes either side of the Standard; the branches can be securely tied to this when they are long enough.

● The technique I prefer, is to use soft string, tied near the end of the arching branches and pulled in before securing to the stake underneath. It can be difficult to achieve this, especially if the variety is very thorny, but worth it for the sake of appearance.

● Alternatively the strings can be pegged to the ground or weighted with stones, but once again the image becomes unnatural.

Check regularly that ties are not rubbing against the stem and that the stake is still firmly held in the ground and is not weakening at the base.

Using a training umbrella to secure the branches of Weeping standards.

how to revive roses

Pruning the rose hedge

I have already mentioned the importance of making cuts above a bud in several places and keeping them clean, but when it comes to tackling a hedge this principle is far from practical. If the hedge is of Species roses or a collection of different varieties, I would not advocate that it be pruned in any uniform manner, rather look on it as a boundary made up of individual plants and tidied only when necessary. Rugosa hedges, or hedges made up of a solitary variety, can be treated in a similar manner to the privet or beech hedge and can be pruned to the same height or width all along. This can be done using shears or a powered hedge-trimmer. Little bits of dieback will occur, but the density of the hedge and clothing of leaves and flowers in the summer disguises this. Large beds of roses can also be dealt with in this way, if time is limited.

The techniques for pruning rose hedges are varied.

Reviving old roses

If you have inherited roses in the garden of a property new to you, it is likely that they will need attention to bring them back to their best. Let them flower before trying to help them, though; they may not be to your taste, and your time will have been wasted. Or it may be that you have only recently found the time to devote to your roses, and they too may need drastic attention. Any mature rose which has become leggy, with only a little new growth at the top and lots of old gnarled wood at the base, must be dealt with severely. Whilst the principles of this are much the same, I have devoted some words of guidance for each type of rose specifically. In all cases, however, the rose once pruned should be well fed. There are many different rose fertilizers available, and all supply a balanced mixture of nutrients. However, as well as these aids to well-being, a solution of liquid seaweed or other high-nitrogen feed, promotes growth.

If the rose is in its twilight years, the simple solution is to dig it up and replace it, remembering to change the soil before planting the new one. If the name of it is unknown, take or post to a specialist nursery some samples of it (as much of the rose as possible including new and old growth, leaves and flowers at different stages), imparting all you know about size and flowering habits. If they cannot identify it, they will be able to suggest another that is similar. If the variety can no longer be purchased, you may be able to persuade them to propagate some from your old plant before you dig it up.

Reviving an old shrub or bush rose

If the rose is important, and you really don't want to loose it, sudden removal of large parts of the plant may not be the best remedy, and could even result in the loss of a very old plant. Whilst most of it should be hard pruned, leave a few branches at two-thirds their original length in case the rest is too old to shoot. If this does happen, the dead wood can be cut away and another plant, such as a sweet pea, can be grown through the top-heavy branches that remain. If not so important, cut back the whole plant to a third of its height. Then prune away all the growth that is dead and remove some of the central growth with a pair of loppers, keeping the cuts as close to the base as possible. It is likely that the rose will have suffered damage and any broken parts of branches should be pruned away. Check the remaining areas for Canker (described in the chapter on Pests and Diseases), cutting the branch away to beyond the affected area. Although unlikely, there may possibly be a young shoot or two originating somewhere near the base; these should be pruned harder, as they will sprout new shoots more easily than older ones. Finally, take care to feed well.

Reviving an old climbing rose

A climbing rose that has been in place for some years without attention, will be an extremely leggy plant, producing flowers in the heavens where no one can appreciate them. It will be extremely difficult to get it to flower lower down, so the answer may just to be to replace it. If it must stay there are three things that can be done. First, try to physically bend the branches down as far as they will go; this may result in some flowering wood at least at eye level. Second, cut it back as hard as possible; with luck it will shoot. The third is a combination of both and is the most sensible procedure. Any leggy growth remaining can be disguised with smaller climbing plants. Ensure that the pruned rose is fed well in spring.

Reviving an old rambler

Ramblers are probably easier to tackle than climbers are, because they produce basal growth more freely. Start by removing all dead, diseased and damaged branches as close to their base as possible. Then take away a proportion of the main stems – the oldest ones – again at the base. Leave about half a dozen of the strongest and youngest branches to form the basic structure. These should be cut back to about half their height and fanned out as horizontally as possible, from where they will hopefully produce new growth. Feed well.

Ramblers flower on the growth made the previous year.

promoting growth

Moving established roses

If you have to remove an established plant, try to do so in the dormant season when there is no growing activity. Cut the plant back heavily but sensibly to about half its original size for ease of handling. When it is dug up, keep as large a root ball as is possible and retain as much soil around the roots as you can. This is best achieved by creating a trench around the rose before removing it. It can be pushed onto one side, so that the deepest roots can be sliced through with the spade and then pushed in the opposite direction for the same procedure. Once out of the ground, use a pair of secateurs to tidy any torn roots, therefore encouraging speedy healing.

Study the size of the root ball in comparison to the branches. If there are far more branches than roots, they need to be pruned harder so as not to put too great a demand on the roots; this can be done when the plant is in its new situation. The new ground should be well prepared. I suggest that the rose be planted slightly deeper than before to help stability and retention of moisture. Feed and water the rose well during the following summer.

Roses that do not flower

Rambling roses, especially the most vigorous ones like 'Rambling Rector' and 'Kiftsgate', often take two or three years to start flowering, preferring to build up growth first. This is quite normal and should be expected when buying them. If they do not flower after three or four years, the problem could be that they are growing too well. To check this, cut out any general fertilizer you may have been using and substitute it with one high in potash in the spring; also cut back on watering if you are still doing so.

One or two of the repeat-flowering climbers may also be prone to producing masses of growth and less flowers. If this is the case, cut back some of the longer shoots to just three eyes in summer, and feed with a high potash fertilizer.

Choose a lower leaf joint for the next flowers to appear from and then remove any stem and the spent flowers above here.

Dead-heading roses

Repeat- or continuous-flowering roses, and those that flower once only but do not produce hips, should be dead-headed. For the once-flowering varieties this is done purely to improve the appearance of the plant, but for all others it is done to encourage the production of more flowers. It is almost a summer prune; indeed if the branches need tidying, do this at the same time.

The idea is basically to speed up nature. Naturally, when a flower dies, one of two things happen: the rose either develops a hip from the receptacle of the flower in order to produce seed, or the stem immediately below the flower dies back to the next leaf joint where further flowers are formed. Therefore, it is no good to simply break the flower off when it is over.

Recently there has been much evidence to suggest that the flower and stalk should be removed at the first leaf joint below it – where it or the hip would naturally fall from – but I prefer the traditional method of selecting a lower leaf joint from where the next blooms will appear. Choose one that is facing outwards, cutting on an angle immediately above it; the new flower shoot will soon be seen to be forming.

Suckers and how to remove them

Most rose growers produce their roses using a method called budding, which involves putting a cultivated variety onto host roots. The growth from the host roots is referred to as a sucker, and should be removed before more suckers occur and sap too much energy from the plant.

Misleading statements have been made about suckers in the past, which can be very confusing. At some point it was said that suckers bear seven leaves on each leaflet and any stem found pro-ducing such leaflets should be removed. This statement can only have been made in reference to the modern roses popular in the 1950's and 1960's, the majority of which carry five leaves on each leaflet. Most rambling roses and many shrub roses, however, do have seven leaves, branding this statement incorrect.

1 The surest way to determine a sucker is to trace it back to its place of origin: if found below the level of the union, it is definitely a sucker. Suckers are frequently different in character to the remainder of the plant, and this will be easily seen if comparison is made to the young shoots higher up the plant.

1

2 Suckers should be removed carefully by applying pressure with the thumb at their base, effectively tearing them away from the root intact. In days gone by a tool was available specifically for removing suckers, called a 'spud'. It was shaped like a miniature spade and did the job effectively. **Remember, suckers should never be cut off**, as this is effectively pruning them and encourages them to sprout again. They are difficult to deter, but deep planting helps and is one of the reasons why the union should always be covered. Damaging the root may also encourage their appearance so remember to take care when digging or hoeing around roses.

Standard roses produce suckers not only from their roots but also on the stem. When shoots are seen appearing here, they should be eased away with the thumb in the same way as described for suckers appearing from the roots. Some roses grown on their own roots will often sucker freely, often well away from the mother plant. The same treatment can be given to these, or the new young plant can be dug up and placed elsewhere, or potted for use later on or as a gift.

2

Whilst it may seem logical that a rose is first bought and then planted, this really should not be the case. The ground in which a rose will grow is going to be its host for many years and should be prepared for the new arrival. Although soil preparation can be back breaking work it's worth being thorough, roses will repay you for this by performing well, in health strength and vigour. Roses growing in poor soils will often cope and there are varieties that are especially tolerant of them but the question must be how much better would they have been if the soil had been improved before planting?

The answer is dependent on the individual situation but a rose will always thank you for any assistance.

Soils and Feeding

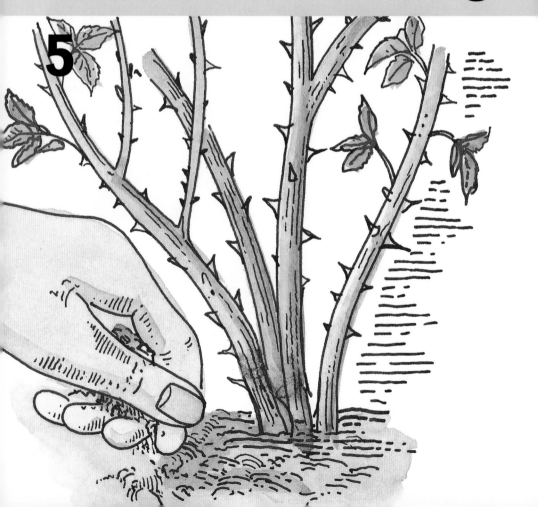

5

Soil types and conditioning

Roses enjoy a neutral to acid soil with a pH of around 6.5, although most will grow on the margins of this. If you do not know what the pH of your soil is, a pH testing kit is relatively inexpensive and easy to use. **A reading of below 7 indicates an acid soil, whilst above is alkaline.** Your roses will be restricted in their ability to absorb nutrients if the soil is in the extreme one way or the other, so aim to redress this as much as possible.

Alkaline soil

If strong alkalinity is discovered, the addition of matured farmyard manure will help; if this is unavailable, the alternative is peat, but as this is a finite resource it should not be used extravagantly.

Acid soil

If the soil is found to be very acid, mix in some powdered lime or mushroom compost. Having said this, there are roses which will tolerate very poor conditions, but they may not be the ones that are desired. We always want what we cannot have.

Balanced (neutral) soil

If your soil is of adequate balance, it is still wise to feed it either prior to or at the time of planting. An average loam soil still benefits from the addition of some organic matter. Well-rotted farmyard manure is best, although garden compost comes close. Avoid, however, compost with a large proportion of grass cuttings in its content; this is very high in nitrogen which promotes fast growth that will then be vulnerable to disease. If neither of these is available, a handful of bonemeal mixed in half a bucket of peat also works wonders. Proprietary rose fertilizers are available which contain the perfect balance of nutrient required.

• Ensure that whatever is added to the soil is mixed in well. Do not simply put rose food or compost in the base of the hole, for this will cause the roots to scorch therby affecting the growth of the whole plant.

• If an entirely new bed is planned, spread the top of the area with the manure or whatever is to be used and dig it in whilst preparing the bed.

Drainage

Rose roots penetrate quite deeply, and hate being water-logged. They will not reward you if the sub-soil is heavy to the point that it holds water; if this is the case, it would be wise to assist drainage.

• Formal drainage can be laid in the form of pipes made of clay or more modern-day plastic, and these are very efficient, but are an extra expense and can be hard work to lay. I suggest that the underlying area of the proposed planting be excavated, to at least twice the depth of the usual planting hole.

• Once removed, add shingle to the soil, which is then returned to the required planting depth.

Rose sickness

Never plant a new rose where one has been before because the soil will be 'rose sick'. Previous roses will have left secretions in the soil that are not enjoyed by new ones; in fact they will find them positively offensive. The result will be a condition called specific replant disease, which manifests itself in stunted and spindly growth that no amount of feeding will improve.

• If a rose has to be planted where another has been, even if it was a young plant, the soil must be changed with clean soil from another part of the garden.

• Remove about twice the depth needed for planting and refill with the new soil.

Rose-sick soil does not have any adverse effect on other garden plants. If replacing the soil is not possible, it must be rested from roses for at least two years. A rose suffering from rose sickness will not recover unless it is dug up and given fresh ground in which to grow. This is the reason why commercial rose growers rotate the use of their land, leaving at least two years before a field is re-cropped with roses.

General and annual feeding

Conditioning the soil before planting is discussed in Chapter Four, and it is useful to refer back to refresh your memory (*see* p. 58).

Once planted, roses benefit from regular feeding thereafter. The best time for this is in the spring, as they begin to leaf up, then again after the first flush of flowers. Proprietary brands of rose food are probably best to use, as these contain the correct balance of nutrients needed by the rose, but other general fertilizers can also be used, and may even be preferred if the garden is full of different types of plants. Any general fertilizer employed should be low in nitrogen, as this promotes too much growth and is high in potash, which encourages flowers. Iron and magnesium are both important trace elements to roses. If using a slow-release fertilizer (one that releases nutrients according to the temperature of the soil), apply it early and combine it in the top soil around the rose with your hands, a trowel or a spade. Other, more instant ones can be scattered on to the soil around the rose, usually at the rate of a handful to each rose, and watered in, or there are liquid feeds, which can be diluted and applied from the watering can.

Composts

Household composts can be used as a mulch, but be careful with them; they are often of the ideal consistency to trap the spores of unwanted diseases which will overwinter in the warmth that composts provide to return with a vengeance the next year. Composts are also frequently high in nitrogen. Although nitrogen is valuable to roses and is easily lost from soil, too much will encourage fewer flowers and a rush in growth rendering the plant less immune to disease.

Farmyard manure also has these properties; it is preferable to dig this into the soil at the time of planting rather than to use it as a top dressing. If you do choose to use it as a mulch, ensure that there is a gap left around the plant so that it does not scorch the rose, and as often as possible clear up fallen leaves from it to prevent spores getting in.

bark chippings are by far the best mulch. This is not so much nutritional, as a barrier against weeds when laid at a reasonable depth of at least 1in (2.5cm). Do not put this down where there is likely to be a high content of weed seed; allow seeds to germinate, then hoe the seedlings away before they flower.

Coco-bean shells are also a consideration and they work in much the same way as bark chippings, but I personally do not like my garden smelling of chocolate over and above the natural plant perfumes.

Mineral Deficiencies

If your soil is low in one or more of the vital elements, your roses will suffer. One of the first signs is seen in the leaves. If there is not enough nitrogen available to the rose, young leaves will be pale in colour and not be quick to grow. Most fertilizers contain nitrogen; check the packet to see if is an **NPK* formula**. These are best to use because they are well balanced; too much nitrogen is also detrimental. If leaves have pale patches near the central vein, there is probably a magnesium deficiency. Epsom salts are the immediate answer and are obtainable from the chemist or garden centre. Yellowing of the leaves could be caused by a lack of iron. Sequestrene is available in more than one form, the easiest being a powder which is watered in; some liquid seaweed potions are also high in iron – it will say on the bottle – and these two can be diluted and applied with the watering-can. If young leaves appear to be going rather red and older leaves are turning purple or brown towards their edges, try applying some potash; this is commonly deficient if the soil is light and sandy or chalky. A lack of calcium may be shown by brown spots on the leaves, and this too often occurs on light soil. Apply some lime during the winter.

* **NPK** *contains the correct balance of nutrients needed by all plants. The three main elements are nitrogen (N), phosphorus (P), and potassium (K); they also contain the important trace elements.*

As with all things governed by nature, roses are sometimes prone to the odd disease, attack of pests or complaints caused by malnutrition. There are also one or two inherent conditions, but these are less common and less important to the race as a whole. Most, if not all, disease can be prevented, and pests dealt with. This chapter explains how to identify the cause of the problem, and what to do about it.

Pests and Diseases

6

Diseases

With most rose diseases the answer lies in preventative measures; they are very difficult to cure if they get a hold. Good cultivation practices will undoubtedly help, as a disease is more likely to penetrate a struggling rose; but do not over-feed, especially with nitrogen, as young growth is most at risk.

A spraying regime should be adopted and carried out from early in the season, when the leaves start to appear and from then on about every ten days to two weeks. Use a proprietary spray that deals with pests and diseases, changing every year or two to another – roses often build up an immunity to the chemical; and make sure the undersides of leaves are sprayed by turning the nozzle upwards, as this is where spores often take hold.

Take care never to use spraying equipment that has previously contained a weed-killing chemical, for the minutest trace can severely disfigure a plant, and a little more could kill it completely. I have included some suggestions for organic control, where this exists, under each heading, as there are different practices for each disease, but a spray from the hose-pipe on a regular basis is a recommended measure as this, in theory (I admit I cannot vouch for it) washes away any spores that may have landed on the plant.

Rose breeders are constantly striving to produce disease-resistant plants, and as a breeder myself I realise that a totally resistant strain of rose is a long way off. We must therefore be content to live with the problems associated with disease, and overcome them as best we can without becoming overly concerned. The most famous rose gardens suffer the same problems and on a much larger scale, but they are still well patronised, and I doubt if visitors to them remember the odd blemish as much as they do the beautiful flowers they have had the pleasure of viewing.

Blackspot

This must be the most common rose disease, and very few cultivars are totally resistant to it. When pressed on this subject, my father is often quoted as saying: 'what are a few black spots among friends?' On this and on all other rose topics, he is the ultimate professor and philosopher. A few black spots are not that unsightly, and the threat of blackspot is not a reason for not growing it.

The disease is usually most noticeable from mid-summer onwards, although the odd variety may succumb badly before this. Blackspot spores can be airborne, and also are occasionally carried from one plant to another on the blades of secateurs or other garden tools. When they find a suitable leaf to settle on, they are not seen until small roundish patches of black or dark brown appear; these soon multiply. The areas not spotted become yellow and eventually the leaf falls.

Fallen leaves should be collected and burnt, as the spores will overwinter in shallow soil and cause destruction the following year. In bad cases the spores infect branches and unless tackled this puts the whole plant at risk. If this is the case, do not be too hasty to prune it in late summer or early autumn, as young growth will be encouraged and the plant will be at further risk during winter. Cut away what you can and apply a winter wash with a mild sterilant; several are available that will deal with fungal diseases such as blackspot. Some say that spraying the plant with a solution of skimmed milk can deter black spot, but I have never tried doing so.

Mildew

There are two forms of mildew: 'pow-dery' and 'downy'. Powdery mildew is the most prevalent in the garden, and is most likely to occur in situations that are dry and airless. A grey-to-white-coloured powder appears initially on young leaves and succulent shoots, causing them to become distorted and therefore stalling the growing process. If not checked, it then spreads on to older leaves and stems and eventually on to flower buds, where it will prevent them from opening, and finally cause them to fall. Because mildew is not often seen until after the first flush of flowers when the summer heat is more intense, a degree of prevention can be assumed with a regular spraying regime earlier on. Once in place, it is difficult to cure, although fungicides will prevent it from spreading. It is best to cut it away and destroy it.

Downy mildew is more likely to occur under glass and is less common. Extreme differences between day- and night-time temperatures can be contributory, as can poor ventilation. Unlike powdery mildew, downy mildew is more brown or blue in shade, and attacks the mature leaves first. Use a proprietary fungicide to prevent it from spreading, and remove any affected leaves. Mildew is difficult to control organically; the only advice I can offer is that a well-tended rose is less susceptible than a neglected one, and, if it does appear, ensure that the affected leaves are removed and destroyed. Avoid growing some of the most prone varieties such as 'Albertine' and 'Dorothy Perkins'.

Rust

Rust enjoys warm and damp conditions and can totally destroy a rose if infestation is bad enough. Symptoms first appear in early summer in the form of bright orange pustules on the undersides of leaves and so they often go unnoticed until the disease spreads, when the pustules become larger, changing colour to brown, then to black. In a bad attack the spores kill the leaves and eventually spread to the stems which start to die back. Control is almost impossible at this stage, when the only real option is to dig up the plant and burn it. If caught early enough, however, pick off and burn the infected leaves and keep an eye out for reinfection. As in the case of black spot, rust spores lay dormant on dead leaves or in the soil during the winter, so gather up any fallen leaves and wash the plant and surrounding soil with a fungicide when the roses are dormant. Ensure that a spraying regime is started early the following season and repeated regularly.

Stem canker

This is seldom seen on younger well-tended roses, occurring most frequently on mature plants with a high percentage of old wood. The canker presents itself in the form of gnarled, swollen lesions, often with surrounding dead and furling bark. It has entered the plant where it has had access to exposed tissue at the sites of previous damage. If the stem on which it appears is expendable, simply remove it, but frequently the canker appears in awkward places that are impossible to prune away. If the plant is important to the garden, the only solution is to carefully cut away the damaged tissue. Use a sharp knife for this and keep on removing layers until only clean pith is left. Cover the scar with grafting wax to prevent other infections entering. If the rose is not important, the easiest solution is to dig it up and burn it.

Viruses

Viruses cannot be transmitted from one rose to another in the garden. If present, they will have been there since the plant was propagated. Most commercial growers produce their plants by budding scions of a variety on to a rootstock; if the material they took the scion from was infected, so will the new plant be. Rose mosaic is the worst of the viruses, manifesting itself as wavy yellow lines or white blotches on leaves. There are others but they are of less significance. Viruses are not life threatening, at worst causing somewhat stunted growth and blooms. Some varieties of roses have had a virus of one form or another for many, many years; because of this it is nigh on impossible to find a clean plant. Indeed, we may not recognise that a variety has a virus simply because we have always known it to be the same. Scientists have found that they are able to kill off a virus, therefore creating clean stock, but this can only be done under laboratory conditions not available to the nurseryman. As a rose with a virus is not contagious, the best way to deal with it is simply to ignore the fact that it has it and enjoy it simply for what it is.

Pests

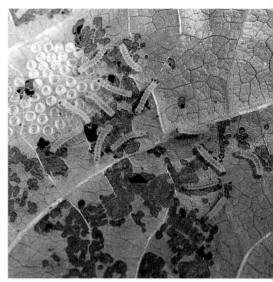

Aphids

Aphids, including the well-known green-fly, will soon spoil a crop of flowers, if the infestation is bad enough. They settle in large numbers and multiply rapidly on buds and young tender shoots, where they suck the sap and cause distortion. They leave behind a secretion called honeydew, which is very sticky to touch and attracts a revolting blackish grey fungus called 'sooty mould'. The best control is to use a systemic fungicide on a regular basis. This works from within the plant, thus preventing infestation. If this has not been used and an attack is noticed, a contact spray can be used which kills the insect immediately, but this type of spray needs to be used each time there is an invasion. Many of today's insecticides are designed to kill only harmful insects, and leave the natural predator of the aphid, the ladybird, untouched. A method of control which is less damaging to the atmosphere is a solution of washing-up liquid and water, although not as effective.

Caterpillars

These little creatures crawl up the stems of roses, and with great dedication partake of a meal of rose leaf. Often they have been present on the plant since the mother moth laid her eggs on the underside of a leaf; as she will not hang around, it is likely that the presence of the caterpillar will go unnoticed until large chunks of leaf start disappearing. As and when one is seen, it should be removed and destroyed, but when too many are present for this then it is a good idea to spray the rose with insecticide. Ensure that both sides of the leaf receive an application.

Cuckoo-spit

Cuckoo-spit is the unsightly foamy-white substance sometimes found nestling in leaf joints or around flower buds. It actually encloses a young froghopper beetle, which when fully grown will hop around roses dining on the sap found in young shoots and buds. It is unlikely to cause any great amount of devastation other than the occasional wilting bud, and seldom are they to be found in great numbers. The best method of control is to give the cuckoo-spit a blast from the hosepipe before the young froghopper becomes mature.

Rose-slug sawfly

The larvae of this black fly are the culprits. They eat away the flesh of a rose leaf, leaving behind only a skeleton of veins. They finish one leaf completely before moving to the next. The only successful form of control is spraying.

Leaf-rolling sawfly

The devastation caused after a sawfly
has laid her eggs on the leaves of roses
can be visually alarming. The parent
injects the leaf with a chemical secretion
that causes it to curl up and protect the
eggs; when the grubs hatch, they feed
on the leaves rendering them useless to
the plant. This is difficult to combat
because the grubs are protected by the
furled leaves and are not reached in the
process of spraying. The best control is
to remove the leaves and burn them. The
long-term health of the plant will not be
badly affected, but next year it may be
slightly more prone to disease.

Red Spider

The red-spider mite loves warm, airless conditions, and thrives in the greenhouse. The mite is extremely small and is not often spotted, even though it infests in great numbers. The giveaway is the fine web that it weaves between the leaves and the damage it causes to them. The leaves become pale and limp, sometimes almost dirty with a bronze discolouration before they fall. The obvious solution is to spray the undersides of the leaves, but by this time much of the damage has already been done. If the plant is in a pot under glass, move it outside for awhile, and spray it with water occasionally.

Thrips

Thrips nibble around the edges of petals, and carve out sections of tightly furled rose buds. The damage is often noticed before the insect, and by this time it is too late. Control is difficult, and, as with everything, prevention is better than cure. A regular spraying programme with a systemic chemical should prevent this little insect from making too much of a nuisance of itself.

Rabbits

Rabbits particularly enjoy feasting on roses. Baby rabbits relish any young tender shoots within their reach, and systematically find them all as they sprout in spring. Older rabbits cause major destruction, especially in winter, by stripping the plants of their bark, often standing on their hind legs to reach the higher stems. If you live in an area inhabited by these creatures some measures need to be taken to protect your roses. A wire-mesh fence can be used to keep them out, but do be sure there are none already in the garden when you put this up, otherwise you will compound the problem: rabbits produce offspring like roses produce leaves. The alternative way to protect them is to erect individual fencing around the base of each rose, at least while they are young; although unsightly, this allows the roses a head start on the rabbits. Chemicals designed to keep rabbits away can be sprinkled on the ground, but they are never completely successful.

Deer

If living in the countryside where both rabbits and deer cohabit, your roses are doubly at risk. When there is snow on the ground, deer become braver in their search for food, and stray into the garden. In the USA, where the deer are less timid, this is a bigger problem than that faced by gardeners in Britain. Perimeter fencing helps, but the temptation is to cover this with climbing and rambling roses, thus placing them at the deers' height. If a little extra pruning on the outside of the perimeter can be tolerated, then the problem is solved, but you may deter the deer even more successfully by planting the thorniest varieties.

rose ailments

Balling of flowers

In wet summer weather the outer petals on a freshly opening flower often become fused together; the flower is then referred to as being 'balled'. This is condition most often found on the many-petalled varieties with naturally tight buds, particularly some of the Bourbons and the Hybrid Teas. If full sun follows prolonged rain, the petals that are congealed together dry out to become a crisp shell which prevents the flower opening. If this happens, the bloom rots within its cocoon and falls away or remains on the plant in a revolting brown state. In larger gardens this has to be lived with until the roses are dead-headed, when the unsightly specimens can be removed, but in less time-consuming smaller gardens, or where specimen roses in prominent positions are affected, the outer petals can be carefully teased away to allow the flower to open naturally.

Spray damage

If regular spraying is a common practice in the garden, it is a good idea to make sure that two sprayers are kept aside, one specifically for weed-killers. If inadvertently used without thorough cleaning, traces of weed-killer from the knapsack or pump-up sprayer can be positively poisonous to roses. Manifesting itself in badly retarded growth such as shrivelled young shoots and leaves. Droplets landing on petals whether or not they contain chemical will often leave blemishes

Proliferation (malformation) of flowers

This is one of the most strange phenomenons of the rose. In early summer a bloom appears to be opening quite normally; then it is noticed that another bud is appearing from the centre of the unfurling flower. This is called 'proliferation' and no one knows exactly why it happens. Some experts believe it to be viral; it does tend to occur repeatedly in the same varieties, although not consistently on every plant in that variety. But the general consensus is that it is genetic, with parts of the reproductive area over-producing.

The use of chemicals

In various places above I have recommended that chemicals are the best way to control many diseases and pests. If only this was not the case. But until successful environmentally friendly alternatives come along, I will continue to do so. Everyone knows that chemicals are disturbing nature and the environment. If you do not want to spray, don't; it's that simple. In most gardens roses are interspersed to the extent that disease should not become an overwhelming problem. Let's face it; although I in common with most Rosarians, suggest that a regular regime of spraying is practiced to overcome these problems, few gardeners take this advice on board totally and many get away with only small disorders on their roses. I offer such recommendations because I am expected to relay the best way to keep roses free from these factors, and I do not want to lull gardeners into a false sense of security. Without a regime of chemical assistance I cannot promise healthy plants, but 'what are a few black spots among friends?'

Increasing the numbers of roses for use in the garden is a rewarding pass-time and there are several methods of doing it. Most can be done on a small scale with just a few tools. The exception is micro-propagation which is a form of tissue culture carried out in sterile laboratory conditions, far removed from more traditional methods of propagation. Whatever method employed there are doubtless going to be a percentage of failures but this is common even for skilled professional propagators.

Propagating Roses

7

Budding

This method is most commonly used on a large scale by commercial rose growers. It is done at the peak growing season, so speed is essential because the quality of the material soon diminishes; and, whilst most nurseries have their own skilled propagators, it is not unusual for outside teams of budders to be brought in. These people work very quickly usually on a piece-work basis.

Budding can be done in the garden. You need a budding knife, which can be bought from most garden centres, and some rootstocks. Most growers sell a few rootstocks, as there is no threat to business created by the propagation of a few roses on an amateur basis.

In the nursery, the rose stocks are planted early in the year, in rows in the field where they settle in time for budding to occur. The process is simple, but it can take awhile to perfect; it is fiddly, and the newcomer will probably find that he or she is all fingers and thumbs.

1 The scions or buds are found on the ripe flowering stems of the selected variety, nestled under the leaf stalks. A length of the stem is cut from the plant and the leaves removed to leave about a third of an inch (0.8cm) of the leaf stalk. The stem is probably best de-thorned at this stage for ease of handling and stored in a bucket of water to prevent it from drying out.

A 'T'-shaped cut is then made in the bark at the base of the stock, the vertical cut being about one inch (2.5cm) long, with the top cut shorter than this. The bark is then opened at the cut ready for the bud to be placed inside, taking care not to damage the flesh under the bark. The bud is then carefully removed from the stem with the knife, by cutting the layer of the bark on which it is positioned off the stem. Start the cut about a third of an inch (0.8cm) above the bud, and in one clean motion cut to about the same distance below it. The bud now has to be exposed by removing the pith from behind it. Do this with the thumbnail or a knife, without damaging the bud, which is found on the underside of the bark. If there is no visible bud, dispose of it and try another.

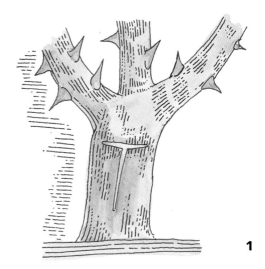

1

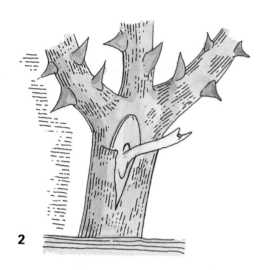

2

2 The removed bud is now placed inside the 'T' cut, so that it comes into contact with the fleshy pith of the rootstock, where fusion will take place. Using the handle of the budding knife, or, if this is too bulky, use the blunt edge of the blade, and carefully open the cut ready to slide the bud inside. The bud is inserted from the top of the cut, and eased inside until it is snuggly nestled behind the bark, with the small piece of leaf stalk protruding between the two vertical cuts.

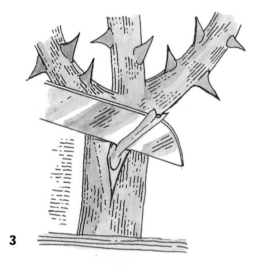

3

3 Finish off by trimming away any excess bark visible at the top of the cut by placing the knife over it and applying a little pressure.

4 Finally, apply a bandage of some description over the cut. Most growers use latex patches, stretched over the cut and held together with a staple. If you have no access to this, use raffia instead; this is wound around both above and below the protruding leaf stalk and tied at the top. The bud is bandaged to keep it in place and to prevent water from getting in. After a few weeks the bandage can be removed. If the process was unsuccessful the bud, will have shrivelled. Provided time allows, another can be inserted on the other side of the stock. If it has taken, however, it soon starts to grow. In the autumn the new rose that has emerged must be cut back to three or four eyes to encourage bushiness. In winter, cut away all the top of the stock just above the new shoot, so the roots serve the new rose only.

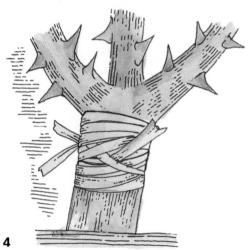

4

Grafting

This method of production is not as common as budding. Grafting is usually reserved for the few varieties that are difficult to produce in any other way, including the banksiae ramblers, and varieties such as 'Mermaid' which can be budded but produce poor takes. Bench grafting is the most common method; it involves the insertion of a length of branch from one cultivar into a cut made on the root or shoot of another. There are several ways of doing this, but it is only necessary to look at one method.

● Select the stock that acts as host to the chosen variety very carefully; it may influence the growth of the new rose in important features such as strength and vigour. By plunging the stock into peat under glass, it is forced into early growth during the winter months, and, when there is plenty of root activity – approximately three or four weeks later – it is ready to accept the scion.

● The top of the stock is then removed a few inches above the roots. A cut is then made into the side of the stock from the top down. The scion will be about 4ins (10cm) in length with three or four buds cut in a slant above a bud at the top and in an exaggerated slant at the base. The scion is then guided into the stock ensuring that the two fleshy sides are together. Once in place, the graft is bandaged with raffia or tape and made watertight with grafting wax. It is also sensible to wax the cut at the top of the scion to prevent loss of moisture.

● Pot the newly grafted plant and stake it with a bamboo cane to support both the scion and the stock in a splint-like manner, while they fuse together. By late spring the bond should be strong enough to allow the raffia or tape to be removed; never leave this too late because the graft swells as the rose grows. The new rose will grow quite quickly and will, if the choice of stock was the right one, be stronger than if it were on its own roots.

Cuttings

Autumn
hardwood rose cuttings

The best time to take hardwood rose cuttings is in the autumn, when the leaves are beginning to fall.

● The cutting should be made from one-year-old wood that is about pencil thickness, although this is ultimately determined by the variety, and about 6ins (15cm) in length).

● Cut the top of the wood on an angle, just above a bud, but cut the base clean across just below a bud. The bottom bud can be sliced off to expose more cambium, which is where the roots will form. Alternatively, take the cutting with a heel, by carefully cutting or pulling it away from two-year-old wood. Any leaves present should be snipped off, and the base of the cutting should then be dipped into rooting hormone. When prepared, the cutting should be placed in a trench, to about half its depth in a sheltered part of the garden.

● To encourage it to callous, a little sharp sand should be placed in the base of the trench. Always take several cuttings of the same variety as insurance for loss; and, of course, if you are propagating more than one variety, they must be labelled to avoid confusion later on. They will root just as well in the cool greenhouse if placed in a deep pot containing equal parts of garden soil and sand. By spring they will have started to root and will be ready for transplanting when they become dormant again the following autumn/winter.

Hardwood cuttings can be placed in a trench outside or in pots in a cool greenhouse.

Summer softwood cuttings

If preferred, rose cuttings can be made in the summer. They should be of the current season's growth and the same in all respects except that they are likely to be thinner and must be made shorter to reduce moisture loss. The cuttings should be placed in a pot, watered and covered with a polythene bag. A cane placed in a central position stops the bag from clinging to the cuttings, and use a rubber-band to secure the bottom of the bag to the pot.

● Stand them in a warm place in the greenhouse, conservatory or windowsill. If watered well at the start, they will not require a great amount of further watering as the environment is enclosed. Stand the pot on a layer of shingle in a container such as a saucer, and water this when the humidity in the bag drops; moisture will be drawn up through the hole in the base of the pot. The indication that they may have rooted is when they start to dry out more quickly because they are taking up water; they will also begin to shoot at this stage. The polythene bag can now be removed and the cuttings slowly hardened off before winter when they can be re-potted into nourishing compost. Allow them to make a good root system in the confines of the pot for the duration of the next summer before planting them in the autumn.

This method of propagating roses is seldom used by growers for several reasons. The first is that a significantly larger amount of material is needed in comparison to propagation by budding. As the source of this material is often the previous crop, which will be dug and sold, the amount of wood used from it should be kept to a minimum. Another reason is that roses on their own roots take much longer to establish than budded or grafted roses; they would have to be kept on the nursery for at least 12 months longer, and the labour involved in caring for them for this length of time would cause them to be much more expensive.

The biggest advantage of a rose on its own roots is that it will not produce suckers of the rootstock, although it may very well throw up some of its own. Taking a cutting, though, is probably the most idiot-proof way of producing more roses on an amateur scale and can be extremely rewarding, especially when the grower of them is able to give them away as gifts.

Roses from seed

Unless you wish to propagate Species roses, this method is not recommended because the seedlings will not be true to their kind. Even the Species plants need to be kept in isolation to avoid insects pollinating them, the results of which would be a hybrid specimen. Having said that, it can be an interesting exercise to plant the seeds from rose hips just to see what you get. The resulting plants will probably not be garden worthy, but will give you hours of eager anticipation in waiting for the first flower and will provide a valuable insight into the work of the hybridiser, which is discussed later (see p. 102).

● To propagate Species roses from seed, allow the hips to develop, then harvest one or more of them when they are fully ripe. Extract the seeds – which may be in any number – from the hip, and seal them in well-labelled plastic bags. Keep them at room temperature for six weeks, then place them in the fridge for a further six weeks, which fools them into thinking they have come through the winter. During this period the seeds can be further stratified (the breaking down of the seed coat) by adding damp sand or vermiculite to the bags, but in my experience good germination is still possible without these additions.

● The seeds should then be sown in a soil-based mixture of at least 50 per cent sand in seed trays. Make regular indentations into which the seeds are placed, and gently push the soil back over them, not forgetting to label the rows if you are sowing the seeds of different Species roses. After this create an even surface by pressing a flat piece of wood or other material (of similar size to the tray) on to the surface to prevent water collecting at any one point.

● Germination is speeded up if the tray can be placed where there is bottom heat, preferably on specially prepared benches containing soil-heating cables, but when this is not possible a heated greenhouse is perfectly adequate. Sheets of newspaper laid over the trays will further add to the illusion that the seeds are embedded well into the soil, and draws the germinating growth towards the surface. As germination begins, remove the newspaper.

● When the seedling has two or more full sets of leaves, it should be transplanted into a small pot containing a good compost, where it will start to produce a good root system and to flourish as a small plant. Do not put a seedling rose into a large pot, as the moisture retained in the compost of such a vessel will be too much for it. Water it only when the surface of the soil seems dry, and then in moderation.

● Keep the seedling in this pot and gradually harden it off until the following autumn, when it can either be re-potted into a bigger container or transplanted into the garden. It will take a while to reach any size; to avoid disappointment, bear in mind that Species roses do not flower until their second year.

Hybridising new roses

In their search for improved varieties, growers continually introduce new roses to the marketplace. Such new roses will have been created by the process of hybridisation, man's manipulation of the reproductive activities of roses. This can be done on a small scale by the amateur and is relatively easy to undertake. Rose breeders have an infinitely larger number of blooms available to them at any one time, than are be found in the average garden, allowing them to plan out their breeding programme. This choice may not be available to the amateur hybridist, so it is best to wait and see what varieties are available on the day. It does not follow that two red parents will automatically produce red offspring; their ancestry will be complicated and is probably littered with many different coloured varieties, and the seedling may bear an affinity to any one of these. Whilst it is often possible to trace the family trees of the roses in question, this is not a worthwhile occupation because little light will be shed on the likely characteristics of the seedling.

Hybridising should take place as early in the summer as possible, in order for the hips have time to ripen before there are too many frosts. If the roses to be used are in pots, they can be placed in the greenhouse where they will achieve earlier blooms.

1 First, select the mother plant. This plant should bear one or more blooms at the stage of being between bud and fully open, when the inner petals are still infurled, to guarantee that it has not already been pollinated by insects. Gather the petals of this between fingers and thumb and carefully tear them away, trying not to squeeze the green **receptacle** below the petals while you are doing this.

2 Then, with a pair of nail scissors or a knife, remove all the **stamens**.(The stamen is made up of an Anther and a Filament as illustrated in the diagram.) The flower is now emasculated and should be left like this for twenty-four hours when it will become receptive; the **stigma** develops a sticky secretion and becomes darker in colour. Once this period is over, the other parent can be chosen. The other flower to be used should be open with ripe pollen; the availability of this pollen can be checked by gently touching the **stamens** with a finger – if some pollen comes away then it is ripe.

Flower parts

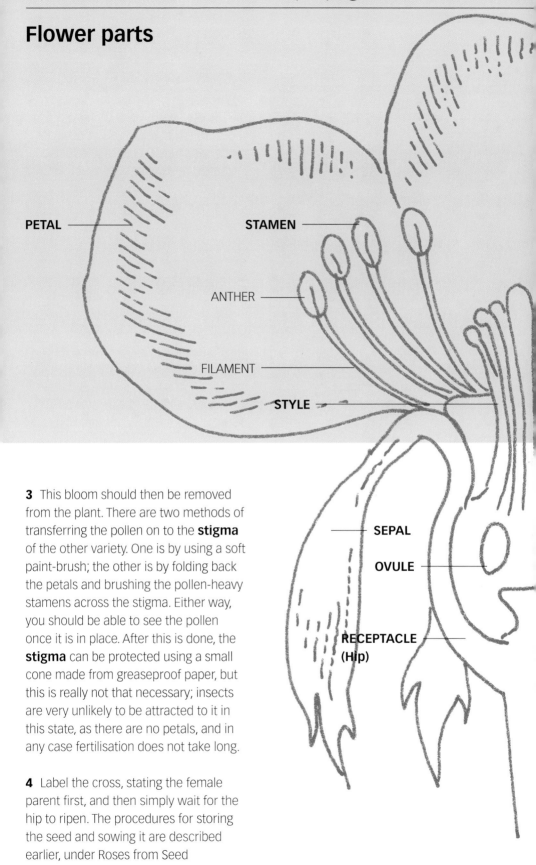

PETAL

STAMEN

ANTHER

FILAMENT

STYLE

SEPAL

OVULE

RECEPTACLE (Hip)

3 This bloom should then be removed from the plant. There are two methods of transferring the pollen on to the **stigma** of the other variety. One is by using a soft paint-brush; the other is by folding back the petals and brushing the pollen-heavy stamens across the stigma. Either way, you should be able to see the pollen once it is in place. After this is done, the **stigma** can be protected using a small cone made from greaseproof paper, but this is really not that necessary; insects are very unlikely to be attracted to it in this state, as there are no petals, and in any case fertilisation does not take long.

4 Label the cross, stating the female parent first, and then simply wait for the hip to ripen. The procedures for storing the seed and sowing it are described earlier, under Roses from Seed (see p. 101).

Layering

Unless the cultivar has very upright, non-pliable growth, it should be possible to increase it by layering, a very simple method of propagation, especially useful for climbers and ramblers.

1 Bend a one-year-old shoot over until the part of the branch that is about 1ft (0.3m) from the tip touches the ground. Mark this place and let the branch swing back to its former position. Make a shallow trench here and include a little sharp sand in the bottom of it. Now pull back the branch, make a small knife wound behind a bud and bury this area in the trench, holding it in place with a bent piece of strong wire. Roots will be persuaded to form from the wound inflicted with the knife.

2 Press firmly into the ground to secure. Although this method of propagation is successful at most times of the year, I suggest that it be done in spring, when growth is at its most enthusiastic level. Once the protruding tip starts to develop, the stem between the two now co-existing plants can be cut. The new rose can be transplanted into a permanent position in its dormant state the following autumn/winter.

Sports

The other way a rose arrives on the market occurs when a sport is discovered. This means that a known variety sends out a branch with completely different flowers. When this happens, propagation material can be taken from the stem so that it can be budded and grown on trial. If it is considered to be a good rose, it can be named and introduced. An example of this is the rose 'Kathleen Harrop' which sported from 'Zéphirine Drouhin' in 1919 and has been a well-established variety ever since. Occasionally a sport produces a throwback flower or two.

Division

Division is a method of increasing plants not often associated with roses, but some cultivars and Species roses lend themselves to it successfully. The only necessity is that they are growing on their own roots. When a sucker appears above ground level from the root system of the established rose, by removing it with some root attached you have a new rose plant.

Albas and Rugosa are often free suckering as are many of the Species roses. It is not unusual in very old gardens to find suckers of a variety encompassing a large area when often the original plant has long since ceased to exist. Rather like strawberry runners, that once happily rooted, throw another runner out in a different direction, the roots of a sucker further grow to throw up another elsewhere.

Invariably there are places that would be much improved by the addition of a rose, but the conditions may be poor, for example, too much shade or poor soil. In this chapter I briefly describe some of the best varieties for the most common awkward situations. These are by no means all the roses that are suitable, and I have left many of my favourites out in the interest of space; others are to be found in catalogues and rose encyclopedias.

Dates shown are the dates of introduction where known.

Sizes given are the height before spread and are the best estimate available; in different gardens and climates they may vary a little.

Roses for Particular Situations

8

Climbing and rambling roses

For north-facing situations

The north wall is a difficult place to get roses to bloom. Open to the elements, chosen varieties need to be tough. Make sure they are given a good start at the time of planting and choose brightly coloured varieties.

Félicité Perpétue

Introduced: 1827
*Height before spread:*15x10ft (4.5x3m)
A refined rambler which bears pompon creamy-white flowers, in clusters. Also has the benefit of being almost evergreen.

Mme. Alfred Carrière

Introduced: 1879
*Height before spread:*12x10ft (3.5x3m)
A beautiful rose with double, blushed-white, highly scented flowers. Vigorous with a tolerance of poor soil and a capability to flower into early autumn.

Mermaid

Introduced: 1917
*Height before spread:*30x25ft (9x7.5m)
Large, single, lemon blooms with a coronet of amber anthers appear in abundance throughout the summer months against lush foliage on well-armed stems.

Parkdirektor Riggers

Introduced: 1957
*Height before spread:*10x6ft (3 x1.8m)
A modern climber, producing open, deep red to crimson flowers on a very healthy plant. Also tolerates shade and poor soil.

'Mme. Alfred Carrière'

Zéphirine Drouhin

Introduced: 1957
*Height before spread:*10x6ft (3x1.8m)
A sentimental favourite of mine, this Bourbon climber is completely thornless and produces flowers well into the autumn. Blooms are semi-double, cerise pink, and exude a heady fragrance. Also consider its sport 'Kathleen Harrop', which shares all its attributes, but is a softer shell pink. If this rose has a fault, it is a susceptibility to mildew but I can overlook that.

Other varieties to look out for are:

'Antique'	'Golden Showers'
'Cécile Brunner Climber'	'Mrs Herbert Stevens'
'Coral Dawn'	'New Dawn'
'Félicité Perpétue'	'Veilchenblau'
'Ghislaine de Féligonde'	

For shaded places

As with the north wall, it can be difficult to persuade a rose to bloom in the shade. The following, though, should do quite well in shady areas of the garden. If the area is very dark, choose a white or yellow variety to brighten it up.

Albéric Barbier

Introduced: 1921
*Height before spread:*15x8ft (4.5x2.5m)
A once-flowering Wichuraiana with super muddled and, when open, flat blooms, of white-tinged yellow. Some find it to be scented. The foliage is dark and glossy.

Blush Noisette

*Introduced:*18th century
*Height before spread:*7x4ft (2x1.2m)
 An excellent rose that I like more each year. Flowers are blush-pink, fading with age to lavender-white. They are semi-double, in clusters and are present summer long;18th century.

'Souvenier du Dr. Jamain'

Gardenia

Introduced: 1899
*Height before spread:*20x15ft (6x4.5m)
Another of my favourites, the perfume from this Wichuraiana rambler is wonderful, citrusy and better than the plant from which its name was taken. Flowers are flat and quartered in a creamy-lemon shade against a backdrop of dark glossy leaves. Although mainly summer flowering, the mature plant produces some blooms later on.

Karlsruhe

Introduced: 1957
*Height before spread:*15x10ft (4.5x3m)
Although not well known, this is an excellent climber. Flowers in an almost quartered, old-fashioned style are fully double, deep rose-pink and slightly scented, appearing repeatedly throughout the season. Foliage is highly glossy and healthy.

Souvenir du Docteur Jamain

Introduced: 1865
*Height before spread:*10x7ft (3x2m)
This variety not only tolerates shady places, it is better for them, because the luxurious deep port-red colour of the flowers is easily scorched in the sun. A heady perfume completes the delights of this rose which is best on a pillar.

Other varieties suitable for shade include:

'Albéric Barbier'   'Mme Caroline
'Alchemist'   Testout'
'Bantry Bay'   'Mme Grégoire
'Chevy Chase'   Staechelin',
'Francis E. Lester'   'Schoolgirl'
'Leverkusen'   'The Garland'

For poor soil

Always improve the soil as much as possible before planting; even if there is still
some doubt as to the quality of the soil,
these roses can cope with it.

Apple Blossom

Introduced: 1932
Height before spread: 10x6ft (3x1.8m)
A medium-sized rambler with large
trusses of apple-blossom-like pink
flowers.

Breath of Life

Introduced: 1981
Height before spread: 10x6ft (3x1.8m)
Large, double, bright apricot flowers on a
medium-sized modern climber.

Dublin Bay

Introduced: 1976
Height before spread: 7x5ft (2x1.5m)
Double, bright crimson flowers on a
medium-sized climber with good dark
foliage.

Leverkusen

Introduced: 1954
Height before spread: 10x8ft (3x2.5m)
Fully double, clear yellow flowers on a
healthy, dense and strong climber.

New Dawn

Introduced: 1930
Height before spread: 10x8ft (3x2.5m)
One of the most abundant and reliable
climbers with double, soft pink, scented
flowers.

'New Dawn'

'Breath of Life'

Others tolerant of poor soil include:

'Alchemist'
'Cupid'
'Compassion'
'Eden Rose '88'
'Ena Harkness
 climber'

'Laura Louisa'
'Marigold'
'Paul's Lemon
 Pillar'

For climbing into trees

I like to see white roses in trees because they stand out against the leaves of their host, but many colours are available. Do not be surprised if they don't flower for a year or two; in this time they put a good deal of their energy into growing.

Kiftsgate

Introduced: 1954
Height before spread: 30x20ft (9x6m)
A famous and extremely fast-growing rambler with single, white flowers borne in clusters.

Lawrence Johnston

Introduced: 1900
Height before spread: 25x20ft (7.5x6m)
Semi-double flowers are bright yellow, displayed en masse in mid-summer.

Rambling Rector

Introduced:
Height before spread: 20x15ft (6x4.5m)
A very old variety, also known as Shakespeare's Musk. Perfumed flowers are double, white and borne in clusters; of considerable age.

Sir Cedric Morris

Introduced: 1979
Height before spread: 30x20ft (9x6m)
A fantastic rose with very grey-green leaves. Single flowers are white and scented, followed by hips.

Other good tree climbers include:

'Astra Desmond'
'Desprez à Fleurs Jaune'
'Easleas Golden Rambler'
'Ethel'
'Evangeline'

'La Mortola'
'Paul's Himalayan Musk'
Rosa mulliganii
Climbing 'Cécile Brunner'

'Cécile Brunner'

For the smaller garden

Even the tiniest garden has space for a smaller climber, against the wall of the house for example. If grown against an existing support they actually take up less space than a shrub rose because they grow taller rather than broader.

Céline Forrestier

Introduced: 1842
Height before spread: 6x4ft (1.8x1.2m)
A beautiful and fragrant Noisette with large flowers of lemon yellow. Continuous flowering.

'Kathleen Harrop'

Ghislaine de Féligonde

Introduced: 1916
Height before spread: 8x8ft (2.5x2.5m)
Small orange-yellow flowers are double and borne in clusters. This is a very pretty rambler of small proportions with the added benefit of being almost thornless. Flowers on and off all summer.

Kathleen Harrop

Introduced: 1919
Height before spread: 10x6ft (3x1.8m)
Completely thorn-free stems produce deliciously fragrant shell-pink flowers until early autumn.

Meg

Introduced: 1954
Height before spread: 8x4ft (2.5x1.2m)
A beautiful rose; semi-single flowers are a refined mixture of apricot and buff, opening flat with proud stamens.

Swan Lake

Introduced: 1968
Height before spread: 8x6ft (2.5x1.8m)
Fully double, shapely flowers are white suffused with pink, set off by dark green foliage.

Other varieties to consider are:

'Aloha'
'Dixieland Linda'
'Goldfinch',
'Narrow Water'

'Phyllis Bide'
'White Cockade'
'Zéphirine Drouhin'

For the scented garden

To repeat a phrase often used in our nursery, 'there are roses for noses and noses for roses'. In other words, a rose that is found to be scented by one person may seem completely devoid of scent to another. The varieties I include here are indisputable, at least until I am told otherwise.

'Aloha'

Aloha

Introduced: 1949
Height before spread: 10x6ft (3x1.8m)
A rose with sumptuous fully double, rose-pink flowers that are heavily perfumed. Compact and upright in growth.

Blairi No. 2

Introduced: 1845
Height before spread: 12x8ft (3.5x2.5m)
A climbing Bourbon with large blooms that are soft pink with deeper shades towards the centre.

Gloire de Dijon

Introduced: 1853
Height before spread: 12x8ft (3.5x2.5m)
A vigorous old Tea with large, full flowers of soft orange to buff. Repeats well.

Guinée

Introduced: 1938
Height before spread: 15x8ft (4.5x2.5m)
Full flowers held on long stems are deep velvety red and emit a delicious perfume.

Sombreuil

Introduced: 1850
Height before spread: 8x5ft (2.5x1.5m)
Another Tea rose with very full white flowers sometimes tinged pink, but not for an exposed situation.

Other scented varieties are:

'Awakening',
'Compassion',
'Gardenia'
'Lady Hillingdon climber'
'Mme Grégoire Staechelin'

'Paul Lédé'
'Schoolgirl'
'Zéphirine Drouhin'

For the greenhouse or cool conservatory

The varieties that best suit being grown in this way tend to be older ones, as breeders do not introduce un-hardy varieties today. Roses grown inside can be extremely rewarding, especially if scented.

Devoniensis
Introduced: 1858
Height before spread: 12x7ft (3.5x2m)
Large blooms are creamy white, sometimes blushed pink and heavily perfumed.

Lamarque
Introduced: 1830
Height before spread: 15x8ft (4.5x2.5m)
As this rose does not survive the cold well, it should be grown inside where its beautiful, pure white, scented flowers can be fully appreciated.

Maréchal Niel
Introduced: 1864
Height before spread: 15x8ft (4.5x2.5m)
Large, full flowers, which exude a lovely aroma, are golden yellow and prolific. The blooms will cascade down if grown under the roof.

Rosa banksiae lutea
Introduced: pre-1824
Height before spread: 20x11ft (6x3.5m)
Early flowering, this interesting variety bears masses of tiny banana-yellow blooms on thornless branches. Not always easy to come by, as is difficult to propagate.

William Allen Richardson
Introduced: 1878
Height before spread: 15x8ft (4.5 x 2.5m)
Buff to apricot flowers are medium sized and muddled. Foliage dark and young growth copper coloured;

A few more worth considering are:

'Crépuscule' 'Niphetos'
'Duchesse
   d'Auerstädt'

'Maréchal Niel'

Worth growing for the ornamental value of hips

Roses should not be grown only for their flowers. There are varieties that have a great deal to offer in the form of hips and autumn foliage.

Cupid Soft

Introduced: 1915
Height before spread: 12x6ft (3.5x1.8m)
peachy-pink flowers are single with a coronet of gold anthers. Although seldom bearing many blooms at any one time, the autumn display of hips proves that it really did have quite a few. Hips are fat and round, light orange in colour.

Francis E. Lester

Introduced: 1946
Height before spread: 15x10ft (4.5x3m)
Clusters of white flowers, edged in pink, are produced in mid-summer, followed by corymbs of small dainty hips.

Mme. Grégoire Staechelin

Introduced: 1927
Height before spread: 15x10 ft (4.5x3m)
After early flowers, which are large, soft pink and perfumed, this rose produces interesting pear-shaped hips.

Rosa helenae

Introduced: 1907
Height before spread: 20x15 ft (6x4.5m)
Very beautiful white flowers in big clusters and stunning small, bright hips that hang in bunches.

Wedding Day

Introduced: 1907
Height before spread: 30x15ft (9x4.5m)
This variety is close to Rosa helenae in all its attributes, except that it has glossier foliage and gets to bigger proportions. The hips are also similar, being small and borne in clusters.

Other hip-bearing climbers and ramblers are:

'Kiftsgate'
Rosa mulliganii

'Sir Cedric Morris'
'Treasure Trove'

Rosa helenae

shrub and bush roses

For shaded places

Few roses will grow in total darkness, but the ones below will thrive in the shade to some degree, either dappled or for part of the day.

Autumn Sunset
Introduced: 1968
Height before spread: 6x4ft (1.8x1.2m)
An excellent rose with deep golden-yellow flowers touched with orange shades.

Fritz Nobis
Introduced: 1940
Height before spread: 5x4ft (1.5x1.2m)
Scented, double but loose flowers of salmon pink appear in a mass display during mid-summer on a well-proportioned plant.

Maiden's Blush
Introduced: 15th century
Height before spread: 5x5ft (1.5x1.5m)
Great One of the beautiful Albas, with powder-pink flowers that emit a lovely perfume on a dense plant with grey-green leave.

Norwich Union
Introduced: 1975
Height before spread:
1½ x 1½ ft (0.5 x 0.5m)
One of the few modern bedding roses that will tolerate any degree of shade, a shorter variety in clear yellow.

White Pet
Introduced: 1910
Height before spread: 3x2ft (1x0.5m)
From pink-tinged buds the flowers emerge as little white pompons. A low-growing rose with small dark leaves;

Also tolerating shade are:

'Alfred de Dalmas'	'Mme. Isaac
'Buff Beauty'	Pereire'
'Louise Odier'	'Pearl Drift'
	'The Fairy'

'Fritz Nobis'

For poorer soil

The following varieties tolerate poorer soils; if well fed, they will do better still.

Amy Robsart
Introduced: 1894
Height before spread: 10x8 ft (3x2.5m)
Semi-double, deep pink flowers give a mass display in mid-summer on a vigorous plant of large proportions.

'Frühlings Morgen'

'Blanc Double de Coubert'

Blanc Double de Coubert
Introduced: 1892
Height before spread: 5x4ft (1.5x1.2m)
This Rugosa variety has semi-double, pure white flowers and tough leathery leaves. Nearly all this group will grow in poor soil.

Fantin Latour
Introduced: 1900
Height before spread: 5x4ft (1.5x1.2m)
Beautiful double, soft pink flowers are produced in one flush on a large plant.

Frühligsmorgen
Introduced: 1942
Height before spread: 6x4 ft (1.8x1.2m)
Most Pimpinellifolias cope with poor soil; this one has single flowers of mid-pink with yellow in the centre.

Margaret Merril
Introduced: 1977
Height before spread: 2x½ 2ft (0.8x 0.6m)
This Floribunda has quite small shapely flowers of satin pink that are perfumed.

As well as members of the Rugosa and Pimpinellifolia families consider varieties: such as:

'Ballerina'	'Diamond Jubilee'
'Centenaire de Lourdes'	'Nevada'
	'Scharlachglut'
'Comte de Chambord'	

For Hedges

A rose hedge can comprise singular varieties, mixed varieties from the same family, or for informality can be a mixture of different shrub roses. The ones mentioned here can be used in any of these ways. Resist buying roses advertised in the press as being the ultimate hedging; such plants are often no more than recently rooted cuttings or understocks.

Félicité Parmentier

Introduced: 1834
Height before spread: 4x3ft (1.2x1m)
The grey-green leaves of this variety make it a feature all summer; in flower it is beautiful, bearing many full, rose-pink scented flowers.

Golden Wings

Introduced: 1953
Height before spread: 5x4ft (1.5x1.2m)
Large, single, yellow flowers appear regularly throughout the summer on a tidy plant.

Kassel Vermillion

Introduced: 1957
Height before spread: 5x4ft (1.5x1.2m)
to scarlet flowers are semi-double, borne in clusters amid glossy foliage.

Queen Elizabeth

Introduced:
Height before spread: 5x2½ ft (1.5x0.8m)
This rose makes a slim barrier, so is best used more as a divider than barrier. Soft pink blooms arrive all summer-long, provided it is dead-headed.

Roseraie de l'Hay

Introduced: 1901
Height before spread: 6x5ft (1.8x1.5m)
One of the Rugosas good for hedging. Flowers are blowsy, crimson-purple and scented on an impenetrable plant.

Other good one-variety hedges can be achieved by using:

'Armada'	'Fritz Nobis',
'Baroness	'Louise Odier'
Rothschild'	'Macmillan Nurse'
'Buff Beauty'	

To create a mixed hedge with different types of roses, pick out varieties of similar size or try creating a hedge of Species roses.

'Roseraie de l'Hay'

For the smaller garden

Smaller gardens need smaller roses. Make good use of restricted space by using roses that produce lots of flowers repeatedly, like the Polyanthas and Floribundas.

Baby Faurax
Introduced: 1924
Height before spread: 1x1 ft (0.3x0.3m)
A charming little rose with clusters of small violet-purple flowers on a bushy plant.

Macmillan Nurse
Introduced: 1998
Height before spread: 3x3ft (1x1m)
A healthy rose with rosette-style, white flowers, that keeps blooming well into the autumn. Compact and tidy.

Regensberg
Introduced: 1979
Height before spread: 1x2ft (0.3x0.6m)
Double flowers of magenta, pink-edged white, open, flat and broad. A very tidy plant that is continuous flowering.

Sweet Dream
Introduced: 1987
Height before spread: 1½x1ft (0.5x0.3m)
Large clusters of peachy-apricot flowers adorn this little plant repeatedly all summer long. Growth is dense and bushy.

Twenty Fifth
Introduced: 1996
Height before spread: 1½x1½ft (0.5x0.5m)
Semi-double flowers are clear red with a coronet of golden anthers. They are borne in large clusters giving a riot of colour in mid-summer.

Other suggestions are:

'Irène Watts'   'Sweet Magic'
'Robin Redbreast'   'Yvonne Rabier'
'Snowball'

'Baby Faurax'

For the scented garden

As mentioned above when talking about scented climbers and ramblers, not everyone appreciates the same scents; I do have confidence in the following.

Anna Pavlova

Introduced: 1981
Height before spread: 4x3 ft (1.2x1m)
Although this rose likes the best conditions, it has a wonderful perfume, and it is worth giving it a little extra care for this alone. High-centred blooms are soft-satin pink.

Ispahan

Introduced: 1832
Height before spread: 4x3ft (1.2x1m)
One of the Damasks with the distinctive Damask perfume. Double flowers are bright pink.

Lady Penzance

Introduced: c.1894
Height before spread: 7x6ft (2x1.8m)
This rose has both scented flowers and apple-scented leaves, especially after rain. The flowers, are small and single, copper to pink in colour.

Mme. Isaac Pereire

Introduced: 1881
Height before spread: 7x5ft (2x1.5m)
Large blowsy blooms of magenta emit an expensive and heady scent.

Tuscany Superb

Introduced: c. pre-1850
Height before spread: 4x3.ft (1.2x1m)
A Gallica rose with a luxurious perfume. Flowers are deep crimson-purple and open flat to display golden stamens.

Other scented varieties are:

'Felicia'	'Sir Frederick
'Grouse'	Ashton'
'Horatio Nelson'	'Lady Hillingdon'
'Mme Louis Lapperriére'	

'Tuscany Superb'

For tubs and pots

Some roses suit the confines of a pot better than others do. Here are some.

Baby Masquerade
Introduced: 1956
Height before spread: 1½x 1ft (0.5x0.3m)
This miniature rose has yellow and red flowers in clusters. Miniatures are best planted in threes, unless the container is small enough to be in proportion to the rose.

Bonica
Introduced: 1984
Height before spread: 3x6ft (1x1.8m)
The flowering capabilities of this rose are amazing: from early summer through to autumn, it produces semi-double, rose-pink flowers that obliterate the foliage behind. Bonica will spill over the sides of its pot.

Grüss an Aachen
Introduced: 1909
Height before spread: 2x2ft (0.6x0.6m)
Full flowers of cream are often overlaid with shades of peach. They are freely produced throughout the summer on a healthy, compact plant.

The Fairy
Introduced: 1932
Height before spread: 2x4ft (0.6x1.2m)
This rose looks great in a tall container, from which it will cascade. Flowers are small, soft pink and in clusters.

Robin Redbreast
Introduced: 1984
Height before spread: 11/2x3 ft (0.5x1m)
Single flowers with a yellow eye are produced in profusion on a compact, broader than tall, plant.

Other roses good in tubs are:

'Ballerina'	'Sunblaze'
'Cinderella'	'White Pet'
'Comte de Chambord'	'Yvonne Rabier'

'Grüss an Aachen'

For the greenhouse or cool conservatory

Some roses make good pot plants in the greenhouse, where their perfume seems to be magnified, because the conditions there are far more like their natural habitat than are our gardens.

Clementina Carbonieri

Introduced: 1913
Height before spread: 3x2ft (1x0.6m) Full flowers are a mixture of coral pinks and oranges, scented, and set off by dark glossy leaves.

Comtesse du Cayla

Introduced: 1902
Height before spread: 3x3 ft (1x1m)
A brightly coloured variety of pink and orange semi-single flowers with a magnificent perfume.

Lady Hillingdon

Introduced: 1910
Height before spread: 3x2ft (1x0.6m)
The superbly scented flowers of an apricot shade go beautifully with the dark foliage and plum-coloured young shoots of this rose.

The Bride

Introduced: 1885
Height before spread: 4x3ft (1.2x1m)
White flowers with perhaps a hint of lemon and a lovely fragrance. Good foliage.

'Lady Hillingdon'

Tipsy Imperial Concubine

Introduced: discovered in China in 1982, no one is sure how old it really is
Height before spread: 2x2ft (0.6x0.6m)
A lovely rose with a great name! Large double flowers are blush-pink flushed yellow with occasional carmine mark

Other roses for growing inside
include:

'Fortune's Double   'Noella
  Yellow'   Nabonnand'
'Mme. Wagram   'Papillon'

For the ornamental value of hips

Roses have a wide range of hips from round to flagon-shape, and they are found on hybrids as well as Species roses. Each of the five listed below is different.

Geranium
Introduced: 1938
Height before spread: 8x5ft (2.5x1.5m)
This is a hybrid Moyesii variety with rounded leaves, single orange-red flowers and stunning flagon-shaped hips. Quite a substantial plant.

Rosa Moyesii 'Geranium'

Mary Queen of Scots
Introduced: An old variety
Height before spread: 3x3ft (1x1m)
Single, soft-creamy-pink flowers are edged in a deeper shade. They appear in large numbers in late spring and by the autumn the receptacles have turned into polished dark-mahogany-coloured hips; date unknown.

Rosa glauca
Introduced: pre-1830
Height before spread: 6x5 ft (1.8x1.5m)
The flowers are not stunning, but the leaves and hips are. The unique foliage is blue-grey and makes a super backdrop to the rounded, maroon-red hips.

Rosa omiensis pteracantha
Introduced: 1990
Height before spread: 10x6ft (3x1.8m)
This rose is included here because the combination of the hips and thorns is stunning. The flowers are less significant, single and white with only four petals. The thorns are huge, broad and almost continuous along the stem, the hips slender with a bulge towards their base.

Scabrosa
Introduced: Origin unknown
Height before spread: 6x4ft (1.8x1.2m)
Some of the Rugosas have very large, tomato-shaped hips of deep orangey-red, and this is no exception. Flowers are large, single with magenta-pink, wing-like flowers; of unknown origin.

Others that should not be overlooked are:

'Autumn Fire'	'Fru Dagmar
'Bonica'	Hastrup'
'Eddies Jewel'	'Master Hugh'
	Rosa rugosa alba

February to end of March

This is the best time for pruning roses, but wait until the frosts have passed.

● Check that Standard stakes are still in good order while you are pruning and that ties on both Standards and climbers are not too tight.
● If you still have bare-root roses to be planted, this is the last window available so they really must go in now.
● Apply a top dressing of a good rose food. If you are going to grow roses from seed, now is the time to sow them using bottom heat where possible.
● You will now be able to see the first signs of new growth, bearing promises of the blooms to follow in summer.

Mid March to end of May

Top dress roses with a well-balanced rose food when they start to leaf up; follow the manufacturer's instructions, although a handful per rose is usual.

● Start the spraying regime, using a multipurpose rose spray; if you have used the same brand for more than two years this is the time to change – roses build up immunities to them.
● Repeat the spraying process every ten days to two weeks. If you want to propagate roses by layering, this is the ideal time.
● Now is also the time for hybridising under glass, if you wish to try creating new varities.

Rose calendar

June to end of September

Dead-head to encourage blooms, but leave dead flowers on hip-bearing roses.

● Summer prune once-flowering shrub roses and ramblers.
● Keep up the spraying programme; it is very important.
● Clear away dead leaves and remove diseased leaves that have escaped the spray and where possible burn them.
● Check and remove new suckers. Budding and grafting should now be complete. Take hardwood cuttings.

October to end of January

Any time now, bare-root roses will arrive. Be prepared for this and have an area covered for heeling-in. It will save time on the day if holes are pre-dug.

● If wanting to grow roses from seed, the hips should now be gathered.
● Cut back tall freestanding repeat-flowering shrubs and bedding roses to prevent wind-rock before the weather gets too severe.

PLANTING AND PRUNING BARE ROOT ROSES IN THE US

Pacific Northwest **plant** JAN–APRIL **prune** JAN
Pacific Seaboard **plant** JAN–,FEB **prune** DEC
South West **plant** DEC–JAN **prune** JAN
South Central **plant** DEC – FEB **prune** JAN
Mid South **plant** FEB– MARCH, NOV
prune JAN–FEB

Eastern Seaboard **plant** MARCH– MAY, OCT– NOV
prune MARCH
Northeast **planting** MARCH–MAY, OCT– NOV
prune MARCH– APRIL
North Central **plant** APRIL– MAY, OCT– NOV
prune MARCH
Subtropical **plant** DEC–JAN **prune** DEC–JAN

acidity: A state of the soil where the pH is less than 7.

alkaline: A state of the soil where the pH is more than 7.

anther: The part of the stamen containing pollen.

bare root: The term describing roses being dug up and sold without the benefit of being potted.

bud: The unopened flower.

budding: A form of propagation involving the placing of a scion into a rootstock.

calyx: The green leaves protecting the flower in bud.

cambium: A layer of cells growing immediately below the bark.

cane: A long arching branch, often on ramblers.

chlorosis: The discolouring of leaves associated with deficiencies.

cluster: A group of flowers growing together from one stem.

continuous flowering: Flowers appear successively through-out the season.

division: A form of propagation involving the transplanting of suckers.

emasculation: The removal of all male parts of the flower during hybridisation.

fibrous root: The hairy parts of roots.

grafting: A method of propagation where material from one plant is encouraged to bond with the roots of another.

heel: The small piece of two-year-old bark found at the base of heel cuttings.

heeling-in: A method of storing bare-root roses in the ground before planting.

hip: The seed-carrying fruit of roses.

hybrid: A variety that is derived from two other roses.

hybridisation: The method of creating new varieties.

lateral: A side branch growing from a main branch.

lax: An open, loose habit of growth.

layering: A method of propagation involving burying a section of a branch while it is still growing until roots develop.

moss: The hairy down found on some roses.

mulch: An application of usually organic material spread over the ground.

node: The place at a leaf joint where a bud is found.

nutrient: A water-soluble beneficial substance found in the soil taken up by the roots.

pegging down: A way of training shrub roses, so they are broad in growth.

pH: The scale on which alkalinity and acidity are measured in the soil.

pollinate: The application of pollen to the stigma of a separate flower during hybridisation.

pruning: The cutting back of plants to encourage young growth and improved flowering.

receptacle: The swollen area found at the base of the flower, which later becomes the hip.

repeat flowering: Flowers appear in definite waves during the season.

rootstock: The rose used for the roots on budded and grafted plants.

scion: The piece of plant stem used in budding and grafting, which becomes the branches of the plant.

spore: The seed of organisms; here referring to fungal diseases.

sport: A variety which results from a mutation on another rose.

stamen: Stamens make up the whorl, which surrounds the stigma within a flower.

stigma: The very centre of the flower with receptive cells prepared to accept pollen.

suckers: The branches that grow from roots separate from the main plant.

summer flowering: Flowering just once during the summer.

tap root: The main and thickest roots of the root system.

union: The place on a budded or grafted plant where the branches and roots join.

Page numbers in italics refer to illustrations

Beales, Amanda, *Old Fashioned Roses*, Cassell, 1990.
Beales, Peter, *Classic Roses*, rev. edn, Harvill, 1997.
Beales, Peter, *Roses*, Harper Collins, 1992.
Beales, Peter, *Twentieth Century Roses*, Collins Harvill, 1988.
Jekyll, Gertrude, and Mawley, Edward, *Roses for English Gardens*,
    Antique Collectors Club, rep. 1990.
Le Rougetel, Hazel, *A Heritage of Roses*, Unwin Hyman, 1988.
Royal National Rose Society, *How to Grow Roses*, 1992.
Scanniello, Stephen, and Bayard, Tania, *Roses of America*, Henry Holt, 1990.
Squire, David, *Roses*, Hamlyn, 1998.
Stuart Thomas, Graham, *The Old Shrub Roses*, Dent, rep. 1986.
Toogood, Alan, *Propagation*, Dent, 1980.

Photographic Acknowledgements

Peter Beales 5, 15, 19, 23 bottom, 25, 27, 92 left, 107, 110, 111, 112, 114 **Professor Stefan Buczacki** 84, 85, 86, 87 right, 88 right **Garden Picture Library**/Clive Bournell 41, /Lynne Brotchie 34, /Brian Carter 89, /John Glover 35, /Sunniva Harte 40, 108, /Michael Howes 54, /Howard Rice 83, /Didier Willery 70 **Octopus Publishing Group Ltd.** 16 bottom, 17 top, 17 bottom, 18, 20, 23 top, 118/Jerry Harpur 22, /David Loftus front cover bottom, /Sean Myers back cover, 1, 2, 3, 10, 44, 45, 46 left, 46 right, 47, 48 top left, 48 top right, 48 bottom left, 48 bottom right, 51 top, 51 bottom, 52 top, 52 bottom, 53, 56 top, 56 bottom, 57, 58, 60, 61, 62, 63 top, 63 bottom, 73, 74, 75, 80, 90 left, 94, 98, 100, 104 top, 104 bottom, 106, /Howard Rice 4, 82, /Pamla Toler 12 top, /Steve Wooster front cover top left, front cover top right, 11 top, 12 bottom, 13 top, 14, 21 bottom, 24, 115, 120, /George Wright 11 bottom, 13 bottom, 16 top, 21 **Harpur Garden Library** 31 top, 37 **Holt Studios International**/Nigel Cattlin 90 right **Andrew Lawson** 29, 31 bottom, 36, 71, 109 top, 113, 116 bottom, 117, 119, 122 **Photos Horticultural** 88 left **Harry Smith Collection** 39, 42, 64, 66, 87 left, 92 right, 93, 109 Bottom, 116 Top, 121.

ACKNOWLEDGEMENTS

This book is dedicated to the rose 'Maiden's Blush' and the man she so inspired. I would also like to thank the following people for their help and co-operation whilst compiling *Rose Basics*. Firstly, my husband David for his help and unselfish understanding and my lovely young children, Laura and Alexander who, although irritated that I could not play whilst writing, managed to occupy themselves most of the time. My father for being my inspiration and mentor and for allowing his gardens to be used for many of the photographs and supplying others, and my ever patient listening and understanding mother. My brother, for his advice. I would also like to thank my father-in-law, Les, for the time he gave during photography, his hands and feet now immortalised, and all my colleagues at Peter Beales Roses, many of them feature in the photographs and I am very grateful for the help they gave at a very busy time. Finally I also thank Karen and all the team at Hamlyn for their dedication and hard work.